Simplified

Writing

101

Top Secrets for College Success

EB Conroy, MA, MFA

What writing professionals, teachers, parents, and adults are saying about this book . . .

"I have simply fallen in love with your book, *Simplified Writing 101: Top Secrets for College Success*. I love your concise but approachable handling of the technicalities of writing, which is especially accessible to high school students. I plan on recommending it to my current class of seniors and will probably require next year's seniors to read *SW101*. I highly esteem your work! Thank you!"
Janie Barbosa, AP English and Language Composition teacher

"If you want to prepare students for college and create strong writers, *Simplified Writing 101* is the way to go. As a college writing professor, I'm thrilled to see students learning the skills Brown Conroy's book teaches and feel confident I'm sending my AP students forward with the tools and knowledge they'll need to succeed."
Andrea Fryling, MA, PhD Candidate, Northern Illinois University, and AP English Language and Composition teacher

"There are certain books that all teachers should have readily available for a reliable reference. *Simplified Writing 101: Top Secrets for College Success* should not only be on the list but hold a place of prominence. I have directed students to sections of the book time and again and look forward to continuing to use the book with my students."
Sharon Hamric-Weis, BS in Ed, JD, Writing Instructor with the international www.HomeschoolConnectionsOnline.com

"This handy gem rings of Strunk and White's *Elements of Style* with a conversational twist. I didn't know learning how to improve my writing could be so entertaining. Erin Brown Conroy's style is witty and sticky. Erin's less-is-more guidance is packed tight and clear. Any student, high school and beyond, would gain an advantage academically from *Simplified Writing 101*. This book should be in every student's backpack. Meanwhile, this old dog is learning some new tricks in writing, thanks to *Simplified Writing 101*."
Gerald Barrett, poet/writer

"*Simplified Writing 101* lives up to its title—it gently unravels the tangles of poor writing and explains grammar for non-grammarians. The book's conversational tone hammers home advanced principles of style and mechanics in a light-hearted and engaging way. It will be a breath of fresh air to students who dread formal grammar textbooks but are serious about learning to write clearly."

Graham Walker, Former President, Patrick Henry College
"College students need this book. After years of reading freshmen essays, Professor Conroy identifies the most common writing problems and remedies them. No student will ever complain, 'This book is boring, impractical, and difficult to read.' No college professor will ever complain, 'This book jousts at windmills and misidentifies students' writing deficiencies.' Conroy's short and sweet primer is exactly what we need, the grammar equivalent to Strunk and White's book on style."

Dr. Robert Spinney, PhD, Assistant Professor of History, Patrick Henry College

"I admit it—I'm a grammar nerd. And I've never understood why so few seem to find joy in the subject of clear and effective writing. But I have a feeling that's about to change. Erin Conroy's book, *Simplified Writing 101: Top Secrets to College Success*, suggests, "The moment of reading another's writing is a moment of conversation," and her insights bring that conversation to a level students are likely to both hear and understand. She's managed to gather a whole range of helpful insights, strategies, and clues to make academic writing accessible. If all my students had read her book before coming to college, what a difference it would make to the conversation!"

Dr. Mark Todd, Professor of English and Director of the MFA in Creative Writing at Western State Colorado University

"Erin taught writing in Cornerstone University's Professional & Graduate Studies division for many years. Many of our adult students decide to return to school and complete their degree after being away for formal education for 5, 10 or 15 years+. They return to the classroom with apprehension, unsure of their written communication skills. With what's inside this book, Erin reduced the anxiety in the classroom, brought easy understanding to the students, and made the learning fun. Thank you, Erin, for creating *Simplified Writing 101*."

Dr. Rob Simpson, Associate Provost, Professional & Graduate Studies, Cornerstone University

"Working in the adult higher education market, I see students approach English courses with fear and trepidation. In her book *Simplified Writing 101: Top Secrets to College Success*, Conroy provides an engaging and humorous approach to writing in the academic setting. The book is an excellent tool, helping students learn how to write in higher education as well as a useful resource for professional writing. Conroy "forget[s] the high-falutin' vocabulary that English teachers wade through" and creates a rich learning environment, helping students achieve success in writing."

Linda Haveman, PhD, LPC, Dean of Academics and Assessment and Professional & Graduate Studies, Cornerstone University

"*Simplified Writing 101* is inviting and brilliant! With trademark humor and sensitivity, Erin Brown Conroy reveals that the rules of communication don't just make sense—they're also empowering and exciting. Highly recommended."

Lisa Mladinich, Founder, AmazingCatechists.com

"Using humorous and relatable examples, *Simplified Writing 101* employs practical, down-to-earth language to teach higher-level writing skills—where a 'Four Step Dance' prepares you to write a paper of any length, and 'Blueprinting' isn't just an architectural term. If you're looking for a traditional writing manual or textbook—complete with boring grammar rules and technical terms—then put this book down. But if you want a simple tool that's engaging for both experienced and novice writers alike, this is the book for you and your students. As a writing instructor, I've used *Simplified Writing 101* in the classroom for six years—and have seen the results: students read and apply what they learn, to become clear and cogent writers. Highly recommended."

Aubrey Heki, AP English Language and Composition Lead Teacher

"As one of Professor Brown Conroy's former students, I know *Simplified Writing 101* transformed my writing. Prof. Brown Conroy taught me how to organize my ideas, think logically, and write coherently. I've read many books on writing, but hers pointed out specific flaws in my work and showed me how to improve when I had hit a writing plateau.

Her approach to writing not only combines many of the suggestions I've heard in other places, but also adds completely new material. I am now teaching writing, and I incorporate things I learned from her to teach to my students. (In fact, I'm self-editing my review for sundry words of silliness and I can't tell you how many times I was tempted to use "this"...) Prof. Brown Conroy is responsible for the health and well-being of my inner editor, who now loves the red pen more than ever."

Alicia C. (five-star reviewer on Amazon)

"What a delightful book this is, to prepare students for college writing! The author writes in a friendly manner. She explains everything, starting with the difference between her conversational writing style in this book and the academic writing style used in college.

I don't like to bore you because the author never does. But in case you would like to know what's included, she covers word choice, sentences, paragraphs, punctuation, grammar, structure and form, revision, the final product, and

even submitting and communicating with professors. As an English professor herself, she knows her stuff. But in addition to that, she knows how to present it in ways that are clear, positive, and actually enjoyable."
Margaret M. Myers (five-star reviewer on Amazon)

"I got a lot of value out of this book. I am currently writing my first book and some of the writing tricks and items to watch out for were very helpful. It is broken down to simple, easy to read sections, so if I want to find something specific to make a clarification, then I can find it quickly. I like that it was simple, specific, easy-to-read, and offered information I could use."
Kennedy Brown, Amazon review

"I want to pay you a compliment. My older son finished his first college English class this semester; and he not only got an A on every assignment, but he was the only student in the class who was not required to complete separate grammar exercises. When comparing his college professor and you, Michael said, 'Professor Conroy is tougher!' Well done! Thank you."
Susan P., parent of student

"As the school year comes to a close, I want to thank you—You have helped my son tremendously with your excellent content and teaching style."
Debbie C., parent of student

What students are saying about this book . . .

"*Simplified Writing 101* has helped me far beyond words in my knowledge of the English language. Before ever reading this, I struggled with trying to understand every rule and term of Grammar. After reading this, my life was turned upside down! I didn't realize how easy and understandable English and Grammar were until I read this book. I am now confident in writing something on paper and knowing that my reader will easily understand while also have been impacted; therefore, I have not written the same since reading this book. Thank God for Professor Conroy and her desire to help the world of English."
Gabbie A., student

"EB Conroy's *Simplified Writing 101* brilliantly explicates the elements of writing with style and good grammar and syntax in a personal, engaging manner. The techniques I've acquired from this book enhanced my success in writing during the AP English Language and Composition exam, in college, and beyond."
Cherilyn, student in South Carolina

"*Simplified Writing 101* qualifies as one of my favorite instructive writing books: the book is easy to understand and presents content in a non-intimating manner. I especially appreciate the multiple tips, witty phrases, and purposeful examples within the book that help me remember the funky exceptions to grammar rules. I love it!"
Alyssa, student in California

"I just have to say, your books are *AMAZING*! I love how you make everything you write humorous and yet still understandable. You are an amazing author! Thank you!"
Michaella O., student

"Thank you for writing *Simplified Writing 101*. I always looked forward to reading the book in class because it gave such valuable guidance in a fun, fast, and lucid style. Your advice helped me to streamline my writing."
Charlie, student in Kentucky

"Thank you for authoring such a helpful writing guide! Presented in a fun and engaging style, *Simplified Writing 101* has changed my perspective on grammar: No longer do I view grammar as a set of tedious and dreary rules. I now consider grammar concepts to be helpful and pleasant tools of language. Instead of simply presenting a series of confusing writing guidelines, Professor Brown Conroy compares grammar concepts to real-life objects and situations, making her instruction not only easy to understand but also intriguing and memorable."

Sophia, student in California

"You have made more of an impact on my writing than anybody ever has; you have given me an understanding about things that I struggled with and, most importantly, you have made me a better person! I just really wanted to say thank you!"

Abigail N., student

"College writing is truly simplified in the book, *Simplified Writing 101: Top Secrets for College Success*. I highly recommend this book to anyone writing at a college level. I never realized how much my writing needed some tips until I began reading these "top secrets for success in college writing." Little did I know how error-filled my writing skills were. However, thanks to this book, many of my writing issues have been remedied. I will be continuing to reference this fantastic book during my college studies. Thanks Professor Brown Conroy."

Avery P., AP English Language and Composition high school senior

Table of Contents

INTRODUCTION

Your ability to write well is critical to your success.
Now. In college. And in life.
And I'm not exaggerating.

It's like this…
Even if you've absorbed every bit of the information in your class at school, if you can't clearly, powerfully describe what you've learned back to the instructor, they think you're dumb, that you didn't get it.

But you did. You just had trouble explaining it.

It's tragic. At the print of this *Simplified Writing 101* Second Edition, I've been teaching for over 35 years. And I've seen and experienced the can't-show-what-I-know tragedy over and over. Brilliant students. Creative thinkers. Potent learners. But, for whatever reason, they can't write well—so the instructor never knows how smart they are.

You see, the bottom line is this: In order to be successful in school, you have to *show what you know* in writing.

The only way to succeed is for you to spit back what you've learned—and to spit well. That means every time you take a test and write an assignment, you have to clearly, powerfully download your brain's content in a way that communicates clearly.

Good writing is communicating ideas clearly. It's that simple.

You're reading these words right now in order to become a good writer and communicator. When you read this book all the way through, you can make it happen.

The problem is, to have your writing *clear, sharp, and classy*, you have to know the rules and secrets. Yep, there are rules and secrets. Some are spoken, and some are not (which is incredibly not fair). Professors look for specific pieces to show up and smile in your writing—yet those grinning bits and pieces aren't always shared with the students.

Yes. You've been gypped. Key how-to-write truths are usually buried under a huge amount of foo-foo—and I believe that's wrong. If you're given the information you need, you'll write well.

Because writing isn't that complicated.

This book has been used successfully almost ten years in colleges and schools. The pages in your hands right now contain answers to the most common errors and issues in academic writing. The how-to chapters came from moments with real students, like you, in real learning situations, like yours.

Here's what happened: As a college writing instructor, year after year, the same student mistakes rolled to the surface. Talk about depressing. I'd find myself saying the same things over and over, scribbling the same comments, filling up one more Word Comment Bubble with the phrase, "Avoid ambiguous pronouns—use specific nouns."

We've got to get this right, now. *Before* college. *Before* the job. Before your closest relationships depend on your good communication.

You can do this. It's not hard.

The format of *Simplified Writing 101* is simple: Each chapter has one idea to grasp, and only one—so that you can truly understand and use the idea.

I'm sure you've noticed: My writing voice here is, shall we say, not of the typical how-to-write book. I say, forget the high-falutin vocab that English teachers wade through (by the way, I teach English). Writing should be fun. Heck, life should be fun. So enough already with stiff-faced intensity. Contrary to many instructors' beliefs, we can gain knowledge, laugh, and love the experience of writing all at the same time.

As you read, I have one request: Promise me that you'll ask yourself, *what's the one idea that I'm going to take from this chapter and use in my own writing?* If you can grasp one idea—and *use it*—then you're going to get better. Period.

Every year two types of students enter (and leave) my writing courses. The first student reads the book, learns the ideas in each chapter, and tries out the ideas. He or she may struggle to execute the ideas, but I can tell that the student *tried*. The first student tends to get the better grade and have his or her writing grow better over time. The first student can't help but revel in the success. Success begets success.

Not so, for the second type of student. The second student reads the book, puts the book down, and then goes on his or her un-merry way, writing the same way that he or she has written all along. Right up to the final paper in the course, I find the student using the word *this* (my pet peeve) and making me meander through non-linear paragraphs that put the reader into a comatose state or make the reader poke at the paragraph with a stick to see if it's still alive. I wonder, *what happened?* Was the TV blaring? Was she updating her status on Facebook? Did he think that moving his eyes across the lines constituted reading—forgetting that the brain has to engage, mull and muse, make connections, hypothesize where such brilliance could be used in real life, and make a bookmark for later? Did the student forget to place the new idea at the front of the line so that it could know where to jump in, the next time the fingers run around together on the keyboard?

Please don't be the second, non-changed student. I'm restraining myself from begging. Instead, I'll say one last, "You can do it!"...because I know you can.

Seriously, when you read a chapter, get the idea, and use the idea—you can't fail. And, seriously—don't follow through to simply humor your instructor, or me, or anyone else. Do it for you. You deserve to be an absolutely fantastic writer who succeeds not only in college—but also in all that you do. Implementation gets you there.

Your writing can be logical, moving, engaging, powerful, and clear. Enjoy the process. Trust me. Learning how to write can be fun, and that's exactly what we're going to do in the next pages together.

EB Conroy, MA, MFA

SECTION 1

Word Choice:
The Basic Building Blocks of Superb Sentences

Chapter 1

Eradicate Sundry Words of Silliness
a.k.a. Never use "Never"

For your academic writing to be effective, there are a few words and phrases you'll need to avoid. No, I didn't say, *avoid like the plague*—for that would be a cliché . . . which leads us directly to the first of today's two tips, having to do with *words not to use*.

First, an excellent writer avoids clichés. The writing universe is full of words. Some words are simple, others are terribly complex, and most fall in-between. Clichés are on the bottom end of the spectrum of an academic writer's skill. To write a cliché, you don't have to work hard (or at all), because a cliché is a worn-out phrase everyone knows. Clichés have a place in a special kind of writing called copywriting (which is when the writer is trying to purposefully connect to his or her audience in a chummy, cup-of-coffee kind of way). But in academia, clichés don't belong.

As an effective writer, your job is to use language to its fullest—while still keeping your points and ideas clear and linear. Years ago, you learned that the shortest distance between two points is a straight line. As in the line, you must make your writing straight. You must lead the reader along an unswerving path of thoughts that are written out in logical, point-by-point sentences—sentences that are unambiguous and direct. Your writing must be understandable...but not simplistic, mind you. Academic writers write with a certain amount of precision that's neither meager nor lavish. And while traveling along the straight line of academic writing, it's important that while using language to its fullest, you aren't afraid of making the line a different color through a more descriptive word choice.

Second, excellent writers know "The List." Yes, there is a list of words and phrases to avoid. Strunk & White's *The Elements of Style* book uses an entire chapter (the fourth) for "Words and Expressions Commonly Misused" (that's their list). I fondly call my list the No-No Word List for academic writing. In comparison, my list is short and sweet. In the university and college programs where I've taught and continue to teach today, No-No List words garishly pop out onto the pages of academic writers—making the students' writing ambiguous, awkward, and flat. You don't want your writing to be ambiguous, awkward, and flat, so you'll want to avoid the words on the

EB Conroy, MA, MFA

list. By all means, it's your duty and privilege to read Strunk and White (at least once every six months). And along with memorizing Strunk and White's wisdom, take note of The List here. Because, with the exception of *very, this,* contractions, and redundancy issues, the following list of commonly-misused words and phrases is new.

- **Very.** Nothing needs to be *very* something. It isn't *very big;* it's big. It isn't *very complicated;* it's complicated. It's not *very unfavorable;* it's unfavorable. Be direct. *Very* is a useless word. Take out *very.*
- **Really.** *Really* is similar to *very; really* makes an object, action, or descriptor super-sized. We don't need to super-size our writing (think of the word *really* as extra calories). It's not *really exciting;* it's exciting. Again, be direct.
- **Just.** We might as well call *very, really,* and *just* the Three Musketeers. *Just* is the same as its cohorts; we don't need the word. (Notice that I didn't write *we just don't need the word.*) Copywriters and those purposefully trying to build a bridge of warmth between the reader and the writer have special permission to use *just* because the word is used as a technique. As an academic writer, unless you're using warm words as a *hook* to your essay or paper, the emotional connection is often not needed. So avoid the use of the word, *just.*
- **Always and never.** Unless quoting a documented source or noting a proven scientific fact, avoid using *always* and *never.* If need be, qualify issues with *perhaps* or *may.* By all means, if the fact that you're citing (quoting) is truly *always* or *never,* then say so (within the cited source). But be sure.
- **You know.** Actually, the reader may not know. Such a phrase is what's called a *colloquialism*—meaning that most everyone uses the phrase culturally, as common slang. Again, in academic writing, unless you're purposefully writing a phrase whose job is to qualify an essay or paper's hook (such as in using a story or personal event), avoid colloquialisms. (We'll talk about *hooks* later. Hooks are uber-amazing because you get to break all kinds of rules with hooks. Trust me, it's fun.)
- **Like.** *Like* is another colloquialism. The source in your paper isn't *like the best;* it's the best. Many years ago, the word *like* whipped itself into a cultural frenzy with the California Valley Girl trend. Whatever the phrase's weedy origination, academic writers need to dig out the roots and throw them away. However, if you're using *like* for comparison in a simile ("her skirt flowed like running water"), you're fine.

- **Got or Gotten.** I don't *got* anything. I *have* something. I didn't *had gotten* it. I *had* it…or owned it…or held it…or discovered it…or something—anything—other than *had gotten*. No, he didn't *get it*; he understood. It's not that the CEO of the corporation *got* an answer; she *received* an answer. If you like the word *got* and want it to be part of your life, that's okay with me; I only ask that when you step into academic writing, leave *got* at home, in your everyday conversation— never to appear on your academic work. Thanks.

- **A lot.** How much is *a lot*? Perhaps *a significant amount* may do…but then, how much is *a significant amount*? No one knows. The terms are ambiguous. If available, put in a clear and distinct number; if not, change your words. Besides, *a lot* is far from academic terminology. Stay away from writing *a lot* of something.

- **Several.** Here we have the same problem as *a lot*: how much is *several*? Even though the word *several* sounds as if it's academic, it isn't…because *several* is imprecise. Be precise. Use another word.

- **Obviously.** Don't start a sentence with the word, *obviously* (or put the word anywhere else, for that matter). What's obvious to you may not be obvious to the reader. Besides, the word leans toward the writer's superiority, as in, "I get it—don't you?" Write with concise, direct, non-personal language.

- **Of course.** As with *obviously*, *of course* smacks of self-righteousness and a holier-than-thou attitude from the writer to the reader. Nothing is *of course*; we must clearly write our reasons and explanations, with no assumptions toward the reader. And, to tell you the truth, *of course* is vernacular that takes us out of academia and into shop talk at the back of the factory, hearsay at the water cooler, or, at the minimum, casual how-ya-doin' language in the lounge chair. Leave *of course* out of your papers.

- **Naturally.** As with *obviously* and *of course*, *naturally* makes it sound like anything other than what you're about to say is un-natural, so if your reader has a differing opinion, he or she is left with a feeling of being weird. Your reader is not weird. We simply need to not imply a natural or unnatural relationship. Leave the word *naturally* out.

- **Basically.** *Basically* is a nonsense word. In an academic paper, the word makes no sense. Nothing is *basically* summed up in a conversational statement that includes *basically*. Please—take the word out.

- **Being that, seeing that.** Consider the two phrases not appropriate…and not good grammar. Instead, write *since*.

- **Because.** You've got me here: I know that I'm using *because* throughout this book. Let me explain. The use of the word *because* is a device for something called *Neuro-Linguistic Programming* (NLP), which has to do with persuasive writing. If you're interested in persuasive writing, do find out about NLP—and the power of the word, *because* (as the word helps your reader to quickly own your words as truth). But for academic purposes, leave the word *because* out.

- **Felt or feel.** If you're asked to write a paper including personal opinion, you might be tempted to write something such as, "I feel that the topic was applicable to current military affairs." Actually, you didn't feel anything (unless you had the hiccups when you were writing). You *believe* the topic is applicable. Use *believe* instead of *feel*. Kinesthetic (or body-oriented) people may take issue with my putting *feel* on The List. That's because, for such persons, life is filtered and processed through touch—and it's hard to talk or write in a non-feely mode. Trust me on this one: take out *feel*. Use *believe*.

- **Think or thought.** "I thought that the topic was applicable" may be acceptable in a journal entry or personal reflective paper. However, for sharing a personal opinion within an academic paper, *believe* is still your best bet for good word choice.

- **Done or do.** *Done* and *do* are awkward—and lean toward writing that's too relaxed. Save the word *done* for when you're cooking something in the oven. The Christmas turkey is *done*; everything else in your writing is *completed* or *finished*. In the same way, you don't *do* something; you *accomplish*, *create*, or *complete* it.

- ***Contractions.*** Contractions are informal; in academic writing, we want formal. *Don't* becomes *do not*. *Can't* becomes *cannot*. *Isn't* becomes *is not*. You get the picture. Simply write out contractions in their basic, most-of-the-time two-word forms.

- **All of, the fact that/the fact is.** *All of what is needed* can be simply *what is needed*. *All of the scientists* is simply, *all scientists*. If you use *all*, make sure that you're physically referring to *all*—and that you can back up the verifiable fact that you're indeed referring to *all*, with statistics. For *the fact that*, we never need to say something like, *the fact that engineers are well educated is important. Engineers are well educated* is concise (and quite sufficient). *All of* and *the fact that* are redundancy issues. In general, use the least amount of words, to make your point.

- **This, these, those…and sometimes that.** *This, these, those*…and sometimes *that*…are what I call *pointing words*. Bear with me as I spend a lot of my own words describing why *this, these, those*, and *that* should be avoided. I want to make myself perfectly clear because I can't tell you how many students (and adults) want to cling to using their pointing words. Hear me out. I want you to be an amazing writer.

And to be an amazing writer, you'll want to leave *this* and its friends home.

A *pointing word* is an *ambiguous pronoun* pointing to previous words. (Grammar nerds, we'll talk about ambiguous pronouns in the next chapter, so wait for it.) It's critical that you avoid *ambiguous pronouns* because *this*, *these*, *those*, and *that* make the reader's mind go on a wild search to find the answer. "What was *this*? What were *these*? What were *those*? And who or what was *that*, anyway?" In academic writing, we don't want the reader's mind to ask a question AT ALL—unless the writer is going to *answer* the question in the reader's next breath.

All good writing is about leading the reader along. When you put something out there that raises a question, and every human being reader starts looking for answers. That's the way we're built. If the question is answered in the next line, you're golden—because the reader gets "rewarded" for reading on. But if the question leads us to stop and go backward, the focus is now going the wrong way.

Making your reader search for *this* ("What is *this*?") slows the reader down for a split second. The word *this* creates a hitch—a glitch—a bump—a pause—a hold up or delay—in the reader's smoothly-flowing understanding. Granted, one bump is not bad. But if your paper has a bunch of little bumps throughout, the little bumps add up to a lot of uncomfortable-ness for the reader. Unless you can guarantee me that your paper borders on flawlessness, with no other bumps, I can assure you—you can't afford to use *this*, *these*, *those*, and sometimes *that*.

Unless writing a web blog, a conversational trade book, or copy for a sales letter for bulk mailing or the Internet, save the words *this*, *these*, *those*, and *that* for the moment when you can literally point to something.

Right now, as you're sitting there reading, I'm going to point out something. Are you ready?

Don't write like me. I mean, don't write like me, in the way that I'm writing on the pages of this book (yes, I just used the word *this*…and *just*). Because right here, in this book, I don't write like I'm telling you to write. There's a reason for my inconsistency…and it's not that I want to trick you, offend you, or throw you into confusion.

Here's the reason:

All writing is specific to an audience. You are my audience. I'm assuming that you want to get the facts—the tips, tricks, and requisites to great academic writing—in a prompt format, in your own language. Forget the educationese or academicese…because who wants to struggle when trying to learn how to write clearly?

I imagine you sitting there right now, saying, "Put it to me straight." So, in light of who you are, who I am, and what we're trying to accomplish, I'm using a style designed especially for you, right now, sitting right here, reading these words. I'm putting diamonds of truth into your own day-to-day language, for the highest understanding.

This book's style is light but direct, friendly but matter-of-fact, and straight-up—as if I've pulled you aside and said, "OK. Here's the deal…." The word choice, phrases used, and approach are specific and purposeful, with the goal of quickly connecting. Believe me, my *academic* writing style is oh-so-different. If I'm writing an academic paper to a peer review board for publication for a professional medical journal, or if I'm putting together curriculum for the dean of the university where I teach, I use higher language and follow the content of this book. Always write to your audience. This book helps you to write to *your* audience. And who is your audience? The professor. Simply follow the academic audience's rules.

So remember the list of off-limits words and apply that knowledge to writing for your academic audience. Hone the skill of zapping sundry words of silliness. If your professor is half-good and honest, the grade given reflects your skill. It's true: Professors don't give grades; students earn them.

And though we all enjoy the "A," we know that, in the end, growing our skills as a writer isn't about the grade. It's about communicating well, sharing a piece of who we are with others, and the meeting together of our minds and hearts.

Chapter 2

Avoid Ambiguous Pronouns
a.k.a. Keep "Them" Out of It

Do you remember the definition of a pronoun? Pronouns are words used in place of nouns. Pronouns, by nature, are ambiguous and non-specific. They're fuzzy, unclear, vague, indistinct, indefinite, imprecise, blurry, hazy, unfocussed, and…well, you get the point. When a reader comes upon an ambiguous pronoun, his or her mind automatically asks, "What?" "Who?" or worse yet, "Huh?" If anything (and I mean *anything*) in your academic paper is unclear for the reader, the brain seeks to clarify the information at hand. Questions pop into the reader's mind. As we said in the last chapter, questions can be good or bad. In this case, they're bad. Why? Because. . . .

Ambiguous pronouns clog your paper. The reader's mind has to submit back to the original word that the pronoun stands for. Just as with the *this, these, those,* and sometimes *that* words, "submitting back" slows the reader down. Which is no good. We want the reader to keep the reading-and-processing momentum flying forward. We don't want the reader to hop, skip, or jump within his or her thoughts, waggling back and forth within a sentence or paragraph. If our work is to capture our reader—grabbing, emotionally pulling, and wrapping the reader up into an invisible web that *makes* our reader enthralled and immersed in the page—then it's important to avoid ambiguous pronouns.

Here's a Pronoun Master List, including personal, demonstrative, indefinite, intensive, interrogative, and reflexive pronouns. You don't need to know what all of those strange terms in the previous sentence mean; you do need to know which words are the pronouns—and how to cleverly and clearly rearrange your paper without these pesky little guys.

---

one, few, several, all
another, others
many, any, anybody, anyone, anything
both, each
either, neither
everybody, everyone, everything
he, his, him, himself

EB Conroy, MA, MFA

she, her, hers, herself
it, its, itself
I, me, mine, my, myself
nobody, none, no one, nothing
our, ours, ourselves
some, somebody, someone, something
that, these, this, those
their, theirs, them, themselves, they
us, we
what, which, who, whom, whose
you, your, yours, yourself, yourselves

Let's look at an example of a sentence with ambiguous pronouns. The following sentence came from a graduate student's paper on religious beliefs and prayer.

"When we pray for those who mistreat us, our perspective changes. He shows us his compassion for them."

Wha...? (Right?) In the quotes above, we find nine pronouns: we, those, who, us, our, he, us, his, and them. So tell me: Who exactly is "He"? *Whose* compassion are we talking about? Who are "them"? We can guess that the word "them" refers to those who mistreat us...but it might take a moment to realize the exact owner of the ambiguous title, "them." When we read the sentence filled with ambiguous pronouns, we have to make assumptions. Our brain works harder.

While reading the ambiguous pronoun sentence above, did you feel your brain working to decipher? Did your brain slow or stop? Did the neurons double back to gain clarity? Mine sure did. The doubling-back process might take a millisecond, but that millisecond is wasted time. Put too many of the millisecond-wasting ambiguous pronouns in your paper, and the reader's brain feels uncomfortable from the "extra work." The reader may not know why he or she feels uncomfortable, but the discomfort is distinct. And in that discomfort, your professor yawns and the grade goes down.

How do we fix the ambiguous sentence above? Here's one way.

When we pray for those who mistreat us, our perspective changes. While in prayer, God shows us His compassion for the person who wronged us. God's compassion filters down into our own hearts, ultimately changing our minds toward God's thoughts. God's thoughts create in us new understanding, new emotions, and new attitudes. Within that implanted newness, we are free to act differently—free from the "old" way of thinking. We can now choose to respond in love and integrity. The original "wrong" that plunged its blade deep into our heart no longer hurts us.

Whoa.

We went from two sentences to nine. Mind you, more words isn't always better. However, in this case, it is. How do we know? The writer's intent is now clear. And clarity is the goal.

(Fun fact: If you needed a higher word count for your paper, the new, clear, linear explanation gives you more words. Yahoo!)

But now we open a new box of questions: For optimum clarity, how many words do we use? We know that ambiguous pronouns clog up the page. But too many words lose the reader in la-la-land, too. How much is too little? How much is too much? Yikes!

Here's the answer: Use only the amount of words allowing you to connect with your reader—no more and no less.

But how do you know if you have "enough" or "too many" words? Let a few people whose writing you admire read your work, then ask. Most people readily share an opinion. You can also put the writing away for a while, then go back and, at a later time, read your text out loud. Does anywhere in the line of thinking skip a point, and would adding a word make your reader understand your point more clearly? Then put more words in. When you read your work again, do you feel like you're wandering around, wallowing in extra words? Then take words out. Go back to the intent of your writing: clear communication of ideas for understanding.

When it comes to ambiguous pronouns, the bottom line remains: In order to create clarity, we must find those scrawny ambiguous pronoun weeds and zap them out of our papers.

Does that mean we *never* use pronouns? We *never say never.* The simple answer is "no." Take a look at the sentence in the paragraph just above this one, ending with the words, "out of our papers." The word "them" is close to the phrase, "ambiguous pronoun weeds"; because of the words' close proximity, it works.

I know what some of you ask, *but what happens when I take out the word "them"* *and put in the same specific words again and again? Won't that make my writing simplistic and repetitive?* Ah, think again; I believe you to be much cleverer than that.

Let's walk through nitty-gritty examples of how not to make your specific nouns repetitive. The two sentences below use too many pronouns.

> The company was founded in 1965. Its goals and vision changed in 1982 and again in 1991. In 2004, they returned to their roots, forming its present "Statement of Purpose."

(Did you find yourself "doubling back" to figure out who "they" and "them" are?)

Here's the same sentence, with changes. It's a version without the pronouns, exchanging pronouns for the phrase, "the company."

> The company was founded in 1965. The company's goals and vision changed in 1982 and again in 1991. Then, in 2004, the company returned to its roots. Bringing back its original goals and vision, the company formed its present "Statement of Purpose."

I think I can hear your thoughts. You're saying, under your breath, "The words *the company* are ridiculously repetitive" Yep. You're right. We exchanged one problem (ambiguous pronouns) for another (too much repetition of a word or phrase). *Now* what?

Who says you have to use the words *the company* so many times? What if you use the *specific name* of the company? What if you write "the company" once, and the next time the word comes around, you use the word "organization" or "corporation" (which is another way to say, "the company")? And finally, let's get downright daring and restructure the whole thing, to include a few clauses. Let's give specifics, to set up the information more clearly. Let's take out the pronouns *and* repetition. Watch out. You're thinking like a brilliant writer, now.

Here's what the change looks like:

> Founded in 1965 by Peter J. Smith, the National Widget Corporation developed foundational goals that guided the business for many years. In 1982 and again in 1991, the organization's goals and vision changed to incorporate concepts originating from Total Quality Management (TQM). Finally, in 2004, the company returned to its organizational roots by sculpting a "Statement of Purpose" designed

around the original writings of the company's founder.

What makes the previous paragraph well-written? Ambiguous pronouns are few. New details clarify information. The flow of the information is linear. And there's a bookend technique used: a specific phrase or word (in this case, "founded" and "founder") is placed in both the first and last sentence. The result is continuity and a feeling of completion.

So your ongoing assignment is clear: The more you practice "finding" ambiguous pronouns in your writing (and eradicating them), the clearer—and less redundant—your papers will be.

Go back to the beginning of the chapter and read the Pronoun Master List again. Commit the list to memory. Next time a fuzzy words pops onto the page, hit the delete button with gusto and write a more specific word in its place. Trust me. It'll feel good.

Chapter 3

Don't "You" Dare! Keep a Formal Distance
a.k.a. "It's Nothing Personal"

As you see by now, word choice matters. Words can draw our reader in or push our reader away. Certain words in our language are "pushy" words. "Pushy" is not polite. "Pushy" is definitely not endearing. And "pushy" does not create the mental and emotional connection that we want with our reader. This chapter identifies academically-flawed, stylistically-improper, sometimes potent and forceful, and even loud-mouthed words that tend to give our reader the wrong perception—and take our work out of the realm of "academic."

The first culprits are the words *you* and *your*. In academic writing, leave *you* and *your* out. Why? It's simple: *You* and *your* are too personal. Academic writing is not meant to be personal. Academic writing keeps a formal distance from the reader. As academic writers, we have to be "proper" (think, "talking to the Queen of England"). In particular, the word *you* is a highly-direct word, as if pointing to a person and saying, "Hey—you!" *You* can create defensiveness, causing a "Who—me?" response. We don't want defensiveness. We want to write within the academic perspective: upper-level without condescending haughtiness, refined and well-mannered, emotionally separate yet intellectually connected at the highest level of communication.

For academic papers and essays, we write in a straightforward manner. We address our reader and our topic by stepping back and referring to the issues *outside of ourselves*. We speak about *the problem*, not *your problem*. As an academic writer, because we're purposefully fashioning a place of proper positioning, we write without *you* and *your*.

The words *I* and *we* are the same: personal. For upper-level academic writing, close-and-personal is *out*, and professional and emotionally separate is *in*. In your academic work, unless quoting a source's verbal communication, *I* and *we* don't exist. I don't refer to myself; I refer to *the researcher*. I didn't come to a conclusion; I simply state, "The results indicate…." Now, if you're reading current research, you'll notice that there's a new trend toward personal language. When you're a rich-and-famous researcher, a celebrity of academia, or a writer transmitting your heady information into text for a popular magazine, feel free to go personal with *I* and *we*. In the meantime,

EB Conroy, MA, MFA

we'll stay with what works for those of us focused on getting the "A" in class.

In higher learning institutions, there are two exceptions to the personal-language thing. First, if a professor asks you to write a personal opinion, you absolutely have to use the words *I* and *we*. Because in an opinion paper, *I believe* certain things to be true, so *I* have to speak. Second, in an essay's hook or send-off statement, we can use personal language as a technique. We'll cover the technique in another chapter. So for now, remember: Within the non-quoted material—the material that you mentally conjure up and plunk down onto the keyboard—avoid *I* and *we*.

Another word to generally avoid is *must*. When you tell someone he or she *must* do something (whatever that something is), the typical response is defensiveness. Defensiveness is embedded in our nature. Because the reader experiences an itsy-bitsy feeling of discomfort when told they *must* do something, it's important to be careful with the use of *must*. I want my reader to be with me all the way—don't you?

Are there circumstances where *must* works? There *are* rule-breakers—situations where a writer must use *must*…such as describing instructions for a scientific experiment that could blow up if you don't carefully follow steps one, two, and three. However, for the most part, take *must* out of your papers and essays.

***Should* is a cousin to *must*; therefore, take it out.** *Should* also creates defensiveness. When someone tells us that we *should* do something (even if we *really* should), we get ruffled. And then, when someone who we *don't know very well* (or *at all*) tells us that we *should* do something—watch out! The reader becomes oppositional. He or she puts a stiff arm out toward the exact point that we're trying to make. Oy! No good. We want the reader on our side, nodding his or her head up and down while reading. If the word "should" grabs our reader's hand and leads him or her into the defensiveness camp, let's be wise and keep the reader from meeting "should" in the first place. I consider "must" and "should" loud-mouthed words that, quite honestly, I don't want my paper to spend time with.

***Need to* is a phrase that creates even more defensiveness**. The reader says, "Who *says* I *need* to?" Again, unless quoting a source, the reader doesn't *need to* do anything for you. Better words and phrases include "so-and-so recommends," "research suggests," and "considerations may include."

Now here's an interesting fact about *should* and *need to*: You can—and should—quote a reputable source stating that the reader *should* or *needs to* do something. (There—I just did it, didn't I? And I wrote *just*, too…we're within this book's style…said with *this*…but let's get back to the point at hand, okay? *chuckle).

Reputable sources are our friends. The reputable-source Big Shots can be as pushy as they want to be, and it's no skin off our backs. We come off as simply reporting their *shoulds* and *need to's*.

Then, within quoted material, "should" and "need to" become our best friends. When reputable sources tell the reader that something *should* happen, we *should* do something a certain way, and that we *need to* follow steps A, B, and C for best results—our paper's ideas and arguments are supported with thick pillars. The stronger the statement, the more broad-shouldered the support stands under our ideas. Remember: In academic writing, we allow experts to state the imperative, not us. In an argumentative paper or research report, the expert's opinion is the end-all. Well-researched material holds up our argument; the strongest quote becomes the keystone in the arch of our argument.

Last, be sure to avoid taking an elementary teacher's posture, telling the reader *what you're going to write*. "In this paper, I will…" is a humongous no-no in any upper-level paper. And on the opposite end of our work, at the conclusion, absolutely don't state, "In this paper, I have shown you." Gah. We know what we've read. Just state it.

Why not use the *in-this-paper-I-will* technique (if you can call it that)? First, for reasons already discussed, the personal word *I* doesn't belong. Second, as my favorite high school drama teacher often said, "Don't wag your lips. Get to the point with power."

Words of wisdom: Don't tell me you're starting the paper. Start the paper. Don't tell me what you showed me. I know. I see it. Give me credit. Just craft a strong ending letting me know what it all means, how it applies to my life, and what one over-arching thought I need to take with me.

The moment we read another's writing, we are placed in a specific moment of conversation. Right now, you and I are talking together (figuratively, of course). This moment in time together is a truly amazing dynamic—a conversation across time and space. You're completely in my mind right now—but on another day, at another time.

So, get this: The words we place on the page are *time bending* and *timeless*. How incredible is that?

Ageless. Perpetual. And if the paper page or digital file isn't destroyed, even headed toward a kind of eternal. Within timeless conversations of our writing, we connect with Abraham Lincoln, discuss theology with St. Augustine, enter the snowy woods with Robert Frost, and walk otherworldly imaginations with Isaac Asimov. The written word is blow-your-mind powerful. Let's choose words that communicate well. Speak *directly*.

With academic writing, be smart. Choose words that fit us comfortably into the scholastic realm.

Chapter 4

Use the "Higher" Word
a.k.a. "Be a British Broadcaster"

In academic writing, we take word choice to a higher level. What do I mean by "higher level"? Let's talk about it.

Have you ever held a mongo-sized dictionary? You know the kind I'm talking about. It's the dictionary that, if raised and lowered in repetitions, qualifies as training equipment for Olympic weight lifting. It's the dictionary with the brittle brown cover, sitting on the pedestal at the old library in town, smelling a bit of dust and must. If you open the pages and randomly stick your finger onto a page, the chances you *don't* recognize the word under your digit (let alone spout its definition) are super high. When viewing the mongo dictionary, we either stand in awe or want to run away.

The English language is full of an incredible amount of words from which to choose. Our range of word choice runs along the scale from back-alley slang to scientific jargon (where individual members hold, at a minimum, three PhDs). In verbal and written communication, each audience has its own word bank. Within that word bank, "acceptable" words sit, ready to be withdrawn.

Scholars have a word bank, too. The sooner you learn which words are stashed in the bank, the sooner you can withdraw and use them. And the better your papers and essays will be.

In general, scholarly writing uses higher words. A good way to determine whether or not a word qualifies as *higher* is to take the word through what I call *The British Broadcaster Test*.

Imagine this: A proper gentleman and a pencil-suited woman—our British Broadcasters—sit side-by-side in front of studio cameras. The pair is perched straight-backed and tall, each with hands clasped politely. Smiling with pursed lips, slightly cocked heads, and deliberate blinks, the two broadcasters perform perfectly: the man and woman alternately address the cameras with purposeful word choice—pronouncing each carefully chosen word in a beautifully-articulated British accent. One word describes it all: proper. If the word you're thinking of writing on your page is proper enough to be used by these two, your word probably leans toward higher language. The British Broadcaster method of checking word choice is simplistic and far from scientific. But, as a quick test, it works.

Another key principle lies in the British Broadcaster analogy: Broadcast language is precise. No matter your word choice, don't say the same thing over and over again, only in different ways, using different words, re-phrasing your point, repeating your position, re-stating information, duplicating expressions and terminology, turning the phrase and the idea in, out, and around on the paper because you found one more "cool" way to say it (like I purposefully did in the sentence you're reading right now). I'm boring you. And if you run on like that, you're boring the reader, too.

Be precise.

Here are some examples of higher word choice:
- The man didn't *talk about it*; he *communicated*.
- The woman didn't *go somewhere*; she *traveled*.
- The building wasn't *all right to use*; it was *an acceptable facility*.
- The graph didn't *come with* the report; the graph *accompanied* the report.
- The evidence wasn't *pulled together*; *the source gathered* or *assembled* the evidence.
- The *newspaper* didn't *run* an article; the *news publication* (or the specific newspaper's name, such as *The Washington Post*) *published* the *specific* (name it here) article.
- The *person* didn't *quit*; the *individual ceased to be employed within the organization* (OK, that one might be stretching it a bit).
- The book didn't *tell us* (after all, books don't talk); the *source* is *quoted as stating*.

Which brings us to an important point: When quoting any source, the word *stated* is a key word to use, to make your sentence sound upper-level. The source didn't *say*; the source *stated*. Quotations from reputable sources are vital—intended to be waving flags of importance. Excerpts from experts are our written work's head-turners and turning points.

Quotes are powerful. Properly placed within a well-sculpted paragraph, academic writers skillfully fashion the placement of quoted material—depositing the juicy bits into places within the text where the reader's eyebrows will lift in thoughtful consideration. Yes, the passage from the reliable source *works* for us; it is the foundational evidence leading the reader into a conclusion—*our* conclusion. So…in this monologue about the word *stated*, why am I going on and on, singing the praises of first-class citations?

Here's why: Because within the pivotal influence of solid citations, every word counts. The words within the phrases *around* the quote taint or polish our quote. If Mr. Peter Smith, President of the Excellence Company, *said* something, that's fine. But if he *stated* it, that's better. Believe it or not, that little detail-of-a-word gives a new aura to the atmosphere of your cited content.

Word choice matters. And it all adds up.

But writers beware! We can get carried away with using higher words and lose touch with the reader and reality.

If it's easy to "write under" our academic audience, it's just as easy to write over. In fact, with the worldwide explosion of Internet accessibility, academic writing may be changing.

The Internet sets the pace and tone for many aspects of a written work's style and readability. Declaring that scholarly writing is too heady, some academic writing sources (including university help stations) currently herald a call for conciseness and clarity. Horrified of what is feared to be the *dumbing down* of writing style and content, purists stand toe-to-toe against change.

I believe many are fearful that *concise and clear* will, to many, mean *lower level*. I beg to differ. *Concise and clear* and *upper level writing* can mean choosing a stronger, single word. Undoubtedly, time will sift the debate and conclusions will remain. In the meantime…

It's all about balance. Choose words with power. And know that "higher" vocabulary words can be high voltage kicks for your work.

Remember: *Anyone* can get by using the right-click-on-synonyms thesaurus. But there's something better. It's called growing your skills and abilities…and growing your vocabulary. Read others' academic writings. Read an academic peer-reviewed journal article or two (or ten). Purposefully grow your word bank. Ask professors for examples of "A" papers and see what words "work well" in others' scholarly works. As an academic writer, expand and master a higher vocabulary.[1]

---

[1] And when it comes to your future success, vocabulary building is *huge*. It just so happens (*wink) I have a book for building vocabulary, with lists covering all of the

In the meantime, use appropriate "higher language" and write like a British Broadcaster. Concomitantly, circumvent supercilious inscriptions responsible for perplexing wording and excessive phraseology. You'll lose the reader. And besides, it taxes the brain. If your reader has to re-read your text in order to understand a string of "big words," then change your word choice. We have plenty of words from which to choose.

"important" words you need to know for college-level writing, for college entrance tests (ACT and SAT), and just plain ol' doin' well in academics. It's called, *EB Conroy's Simplified Vocabulary Guide for College Success*, and you can find the book on Amazon.

SECTION 2

Structure & Form:
The Art and Rhythm of the Sentence

Chapter 5

Fix Fragment Follies
a.k.a. Make the Subject a Great Actor

Ah, **the art and rhythm of the sentence!** No matter if you're writing a single-paragraph abstract for your thesis or a sixteen-page paper for History 101: The well-crafted sentence is your powerful ally. Throw away the notion that sentence writing is simple, elementary pencil scratchings on paper. The sentence is much more than that.

Your well-written sentence is a work of art.

In my opinion, well-crafted sentences influence at least half of your essay or paper's success. Of course, we also have to string our sentences together in logical steps of thought. And we have to be able to articulate powerful arguments, clearly explaining the notions running around in our heads (so that the reader runs right along with us). But such particulars are the finer points of your masterpiece, and we'll cover those later. For now, let's take out the paintbrush, dab the tip into the colors on the palate, and begin our Structure and Form section with a chapter on the basic brush movements within the single stroke of a sentence.

The stroke of the sentence must be full and complete. In order to be considered *complete*—not missing essential components—your sentence has to have a *subject* (who or what the sentence is about) and the *predicate* (what the subject does or is). If you don't have a subject *and* a predicate, then you have on your hands what's called a *fragment*.

We all know that, by definition, a fragment is a piece of something. Comparing writing to painting, a fragment is a choppy brush stroke. Though choppy strokes work for Impressionists like Monet, think of yourself as a Rembrandt or a Dutch realist like Jan VerMeer. "Writer-Impressionists" are those persons who write for marketing, popular magazines, conversational works, web sites, and fiction books. Just because Writer-Impressionists use fragments doesn't make such writers a lesser breed (as Impressionistic artists aren't lesser artists). The fragment is simply a tool used for an effect. Academic writers, on the other hand, use the broad stroke of realism: that means writing in complete sentences—each and every time.

"Subjects, predicates, and fragments, oh my!" you exclaim, stifling the urge to slam the book shut and run away screaming. Don't flee! You're an artist. Artists don't run. Artists of the musical variety make rhythms on the keyboards, tapping out symphonies within sentences. As an artist writer, your fingers dance across the keys in clickety-clacks similar to the taps of Fred Astaire, the smooth moves of contemporary Broadway dancers, and the leaps of the lead dancers from the Bolshoi Ballet. Take a breath and smile. It's time for a simple two-step writing trick.

Step One: Find the noun. Your noun is a person, place, or thing. George Washington, the economy, and nuclear fusion are all nouns. You gotta' have a noun.

Step Two: Find the action. What's your noun doing? Is George Washington crossing the Delaware? Is the economy struggling? Is nuclear fusion changing the face of the future? If Washington crossed, the economy struggled, and fusion changed anything at all, then *Bravo!* Your paintbrush made a complete stroke.

Always put the dance together: Make your noun act. And make the action great—which means *strong and decisive*. Place the action right up next to the noun, all cozy and snug, like best friends telling secrets. The phrase, "George Washington crossed," puts good ol' George moving in the boat. There's no mistaking that the noun acted.

Sounds simple enough, right? But it's not. That's because academic writers often write enormous "sentences" that are, in truth, clusters of incomplete thoughts. The string of ideas looks fine to our eyes because what we wrote looks *long enough* to be a "real sentence" (a fallacy in our thinking that we picked up in grade school…more words = cool sentence). But the truth is, without the noun acting, we've written a fragment. The next chapter covers problems of long, "mongo" sentences. But first, let's run through a few examples of how to fix fragments.

Let's go back to George. Here's a mongo-sized fragment:
In the United States of America (USA), George Washington, who is often called "The Father of our Country" and "one of the USA's most memorable presidents."

In the previous sentence, what did George do? Not to be disrespectful, but George did absolutely nothing. The sentence told us a number of facts about the *who* (the subject: George). That's all. In all 26 of the words written, not a single word tells *what George did* or *who George is* (the predicate). Because I wrote, "who is often called," I'm only (and still) describing George, the noun, with a bit of additional information. The sentence has no direct action. Pure and simple, the sentence does not have a predicate. (An interesting note: The grammar check on Word didn't catch the error; therefore, don't trust Word's grammar check.)

There are two simple ways to fix the sentence above.

First, we can take out that little word, "who." Without "who," the sentence is no longer a fragment: We're telling the reader that George *is something*. Remember, the predicate tells what the subject *does or is*, making us good to go.

Here's what the fixed sentence looks like: *In the United States of America (USA),* **George Washington is** *often called "The Father of our Country" and "one of the USA's most memorable presidents."*

George is. Ta-da. George acted. The sentence is complete.

Second, we can fix the fragment by giving George an action: *In the United States of America (USA),* **George Washington**, *who is often called "The Father of our Country" and one the USA's "most memorable presidents,"* **is honored** *each year on President's Day.*

George now has an action. George is honored, and the "who" part of our sentence (the part hemmed in by commas) becomes a "by the way" clausette where extra information, to spice up the sentence. (We'll learn more about clausettes soon.)

Thank goodness, it's an easy fix. George no longer hangs on a fragment, waiting desperately for a wise academic writer to come along and place George's feet on solid ground. With the words, "is honored," the sentence is complete.

Here are a few more practice fix-its:

South Africa, known for its ever-changing economy and resilient people.
This is a fragment. Why? In this sentence, South Africa's economy has no action.

Because of insecticides, the cotton crop of India.
This is a fragment. What did the cotton crop of India do? The cotton crop has no action. (Again, the green squiggly line of the grammar check didn't show up on this particular fragment...oops. Sorry, Word, we don't trust you

any more.)

Anthropomorphism, known throughout history as influencing both religion and literature. Oi! It's another fragment. When you take out the comma and add the little word, "is," a simple fix click-clacks onto the page: *Anthropomorphism* **is known** *throughout history as influencing both religion and literature.* Anthropomorphism (which, by the way, is the act of attributing animal characteristics to inanimate objects) now has an action. Anthropomorphism *is.*

Let drama reign: Make your subject a great actor. Do the two-step. Use a broad brush stroke. And by all means, don't run away. Stick the noun smack-dab up next to an action and enjoy complete sentences throughout all of your academic work.

Oh yes – and did you catch that the first sentence of this chapter is a fragment? (Go ahead; go back and look again.) Before you start calling names (like "rule-breaker" or something worse), remember my escape clause: Since this book is classified as a "conversational work," I can do that. But you—now you're writing with the best of the academic crowd. You're not using fragments. Take hold of your pen (or should I say brush?) and artistically hold it high. You're a Rembrandt. And don't you forget it.

Chapter 6

One or Two Thoughts at a Time
a.k.a. Don't Let the Sentence Run On and Run Off

As academic writers, our thoughts can become like rabbits, multiplying at enormous rates. Inside of our minds, all of those thoughts—thoughts that we *know* need to get out onto the page at one time or another—scamper and stress about. It can even make us a little crazy. You see, the pressure to use all of your thoughts *right now* can become too great to bear. The result? Ideas spill out in a string of two, three, and sometimes even four phrases—and a "run on sentence" is born.

Thoughts are best enjoyed in morsels. Your academic paper is a meal served up in a proper portion and ingested with polite bites. Placing too much information into one sentence is akin to piling too much onto your plate: it's overwhelming. We never want to overwhelm our reader. Overwhelmed readers stop reading. Overwhelmed professors lower grades.

One sure clue that you have a run on sentence on your hands is this: If at any time you have to go back and read a sentence again (because you forgot what the beginning of the sentence said), then as sure as can be, the sentence is a run on.

Another rule I ascribe to, both as a writing teacher and as a professional writer, is this: In one sentence, use two thoughts only. No more. Okay, maybe once in a while I'll allow myself three thoughts… but on average, two thoughts per sentence holds as my personal standard.

Let's look at a run on sentence together. The sentence below comes from an abstract of a research paper:

The essence of leadership centers on creating and maintaining effective relationships that promote positive goals and objectives, allowing us to reach a level of leadership that focuses on three key areas, including the concepts of Emotional Intelligence, Situational Leadership, and personal reflection that leads to growth and development as a leader.

Ugh. I have to read it again. Did you get tripped up on the complete meaning, too?

Tell me the truth: After reading the sentence above, do you feel the stressed-out rabbits running around like maniacs in your head? Without looking at the sentence again, I dare you to effectively summarize that sentence. Unless you have the memory of ten elephants, you probably can't, because the sentence has too many thoughts. It's too long. It's a run on sentence. (Exotic rabbits and lumbering elephants belong in the zoo, not in your writing.)

Let's fix our example sentence. How about this:
The essence of leadership is creating and maintaining effective relationships. Effective relationships allow individuals to reach a higher level of leadership in three key areas: Emotional Intelligence, Situational Leadership, and personal reflection leading to growth and development.

What changes did we make? One sentence turned into two. We rearranged and re-worded a few ideas. We cut out the non-essential information. (Repeat after me: "The delete key is my friend.") Now let's walk through *why* our re-write works. Here are the new sentences, with comments between:

The essence of leadership is creating and maintaining effective relationships.

"Effective relationships" is our key thought. We want to leave the reader with our strongest point. So we want to end on the phrase, "maintaining effective relationships." Put a period in and let the key thought sink in. And, for heaven's sake, use the period to let the reader breathe. Let's go on....

Effective relationships allow individuals to reach a higher level of leadership in three key areas:

Let's stop here. Notice that at the beginning of the second sentence, I repeated the words, "Effective relationships." That's on purpose. Repeating a word or words back-to-back is a technique called "tail to head." We talk about tail-to-head in depth later, but simply hang onto the idea now that tail-to-head allows the reader to mentally flow from one thought to another. Though commonly used at the end of one paragraph and the beginning of another, tail-to-head can work inside a paragraph, too. Finally, I hope you noticed that we changed the word, "us," to "individuals"; "us" is a personal word (like "you" or "me") and we don't use personal words in academic writing, do we? Going on....

Emotional Intelligence, Situational Leadership, and personal reflection that leads to growth and development.

The colon sets off our "three key areas," effectively making the reader sit up and pay attention to what's coming. The colon says, "Take a look! Here it is! Focus! The next words are important! Here's the "aha!" that I want you to remember!" You didn't know colons were so vocal, did you? (More on colons in their own chapter. Lucky devils.)

So there you have it. From now on, you're going to be cognizant of the fact that your thoughts *want* to run away on the page; but you're not going to let them. You'll keep your thoughts together. Put a sticky-note on your computer screen: "No rabbits allowed."

Chapter 7

Vary Sentence Length
a.k.a. Throw Short Punches

Your sentence has rhythm. The rhythm of the sentence falls both within the sentence and between sentences. What I mean is this: A sentence not only rises and falls within itself, but also the sentences *themselves* have rhythm—in the sentence's length.

Some of the best sentences are the shortest ones. I believe that one of the best short sentences in the bible is, "Jesus wept" (John 11:35). What makes the sentence particularly powerful is that it's surrounded by a narrative of middle-length and longer sentences. Then, as if to draw particular attention to the profound simplicity of its thought, the author, John, simply states the most powerful idea for reflection. It's emotional. It's potent. And it's short.

Some of our sentences become overstuffed with powerful words. Too many powerful words actually dull the reader. Oh, I know that our original intent is to *wow* the reader. We want to zap electricity into the reader's brain, impressing her with our expertise. Or we want to capture the reader's heart, wooing him into admiration. But in the end, the voltage of powerful words simply pushes the reader away. What was meant to be potent words becomes banal, as the words lose their influence.

The over-stuffed sentence's rhythm becomes a cacophony.

One of the best ways to make a point is to "go simple." Make the sentence with your key point *shorter*. I know, I know—it seems we need to do the opposite. We think, "Here comes the most important point; I need to 'lay it on thick'...." The urge to write your sentences longer and thicker will make your fingertips itch and tremble, hands hovering over the keyboard with a yearning and desire to throw in just one more superlative or descriptor. But don't cave. Create contrast with different sentence lengths.

Think of your sentences as music. Within a sentence, the words have pattern. One way to create music is through the articulation that words possess: the powerful pop of the "p" versus the smooth and lovely line of an "l"—the sounds in our words are truly music. Another way to create rhythm is to throw in short words versus long words. Within the sentence, we can use

EB Conroy, MA, MFA

many words versus few words, and the rhythm of the sentence rises and falls. Finally, add punctuation such as commas, semicolons, colons, and dashes. You end up with a symphony on the page.

Stay with me here, because if you want excellent academic writing, then this is important. Many academic writers don't pay attention to the music of the words—or the music of the sentences. Those writers are missing out, big time. If you truly want to capture your reader (and get the exceptional grade), then the content—the *what* of your paper—has to be framed within the most basic structure: a beautiful sentence. I'm not talking about creating a foo-foo frilly sentence with poetic words. I'm talking about writing a well-sculpted, well-articulated string of meaningful words—words that pay attention to the music on the page.

Making music takes work. If you took music lessons at any time in your life, you know that "making good music" takes practice—and lots of it. I was blessed to have years of music lessons. Growing up, there were times that I hated practicing. But when I decided to pursue a degree in music (my first career), I was grateful for all of those "boring" hours of practice.

Writing is the same. Good writing takes practice. It takes work. It takes learning a golden nugget of a skill and then putting it to work for you—*practicing* that nugget until what appears to be natural ability emerges. (If feels natural, but we all know it's the result of practice.) And just like with playing music, there comes a point in writing when struggle turns to enjoyment. To become a good writer, you must practice.

Here's a musical tip: Always read your work aloud. When we read our work aloud, the words jump up and dance—or fall flat on their faces. Errors expose themselves quite handily. What we meant to say (and that which sounded oh-so wonderful in our minds, when we wrote it) all of a sudden sounds confusing or trite. When your voice speaks, pay attention. Pay attention to both the words' meanings and the words' sounds. Start listening to your breaths. If you can't catch a breath, then mix up your sentence length. If the meaning is lost, then mix up your sentence length. If your voice sounds like it's plodding along like a mule with a pack strapped and bulging on its back, then mix up your sentence length.

You're not musical, you say, and the analogy of music fell flat? You must have been out playing sports when I was in practicing music. Well, then—let's give it one more try.

Think about a boxer. Your paragraph is a complete round of boxing. The smart boxer doesn't come out and deliver 100% intensity the whole round. He throws a series of punches that vary in type and force. He may throw a series of punches or he may throw one powerful jab. His movements in the round are never the exact same. Make your writing like that. Mix up your paragraph's sentences like the boxer mixing it up.

Your sentence length has rhythm. Use it. Throw a short punch now and then. That short punch just might help bring you the knockout grade.

Chapter 8

Get Active!
a.k.a. Passive Yada Yada Makes Your Readers
Pass Out and Pass Over

It's time to talk about a finer point that can impact whether or not your readers follow you well and enjoy your writing—or frown and leave you. We've all been there: Reading someone's paragraph over and over, trying to figure out what in the world the writer is trying to say…eventually yawning, nodding, and falling asleep with our forehead resting uncomfortably against the pages. But when we wake, we scrunch up our nose and toss the book aside.

There's a secret to keeping your reader engaged and awake. And a huge part of it is something called *active writing*.

Right away, when I think of the word *active*, visions appear. I think of marathon runners with sweaty bodies pounding the pavement, grabbing and dumping cups of water over their heads. *Active.* I think of tennis players smashing the fluorescent yellow ball across the court, sweat flipping off the brow. *Active.* I think of the soccer ball colliding with a player's head, followed by face contortions and chest poundings after a goal in the net. *Active.* I think of flying down a zip line, the ground a blur, wind whipping the face and exhilarating hollers echoing across the valley. Active is stimulating, invigorating, and even exhausting.

Now let's talk about the word *passive*. The visions associated with *passive* are decidedly different. I imagine someone standing flat-footed, with a blank look on their face, mouth slightly hanging open, and an awkward silence hanging in the air. *Passive.* I see hands shoved to the bottom of both pockets, while watching someone else do the job that needs to be done. *Passive.* I conjure up a person sitting slouched on the couch with a bag of chips, eyes half closed, soaking in the third *Lord of the Rings* movie (after already watching the first two)—in the middle of the day, when everyone else is at school or work or out enjoying the sunshine.

Active versus passive: They're polar opposites. I want you to think of

EB Conroy, MA, MFA

active writing and *passive writing* as polar opposites, too.

Active and passive writing has to do with the way the sentence is laid out. Okay, I admit, we're going to have a whiff of grammar here—but believe me, you don't have to scream and run away (it's not that severe). The active-passive thing is really quite simple. Listen up.

Let's start with active writing. Active writing starts with the subject—the *who* or *what* you're writing about. Then, lo and behold, the subject immediately gets off the couch and acts…so the next word, directly following the subject, is the verb. Yes, the noun and verb boom-pow-zip-zap together, right away. The two grab hands and run off to do their active thing.

Here's a super-simple example of active writing.
Jim ran.
Okay, maybe that's too simple. Let's try again.
Yesterday, Jim ran in the marathon.

Notice that Jim, the subject, is right next to the word *ran*, his action. The subject is next to the verb (action)…this sentence fits our formula for active writing—so the sentence is in what's called an *active sentence construction*. Simple, right?

Let's do another one.

After closing the store, Samantha drove to the coffee shop.
Who is the subject? Samantha. What did she do? She drove. Samantha drove. The subject is next to the verb (action). Yup…that fits the formula, too. So the sentence is written in active form. You're getting the hang of it, so let's take our sentences up a notch, with example three.

The 39th ISS Progress resupply vehicle automatically docked to the aft port of the Aveda service module of the International Space Station at 7:58 a.m. (The sentence isn't my own; I copied it from the nasa.gov website.) What's the subject? *The resupply vehicle.* What did it do? *It automatically docked.* **The vehicle docked**. The subject is next to the verb (action). We score again: The sentence is active.

So, if that's what an active sentence is all about, what is a passive sentence? Glad you asked.

A passive sentence switches the structure of the sentence around. The receiver of the action comes first—adding lots of yada-yada words in between that aren't necessary. A passive sentence that's filled with nonessential words (in a backward order) makes the reader's mind pass over—and maybe even miss—the sentence's meaning. (Not. Good.)

Here's our straightforward, *active* sentence:

Jim ran in the marathon.

Now, let's mess it up a bit and make it *passive*:

The marathon was run by Jim....or
The marathon was what Jim ran in.

Say each sentence out loud. Do you hear how the sentences sound? We took a simple, direct sentence and effectively wove it into knots by placing the receiver of the action (the marathon) first. Now let's twist up the second example.

Here's the good sentence:

After closing the store, Samantha drove to the coffee shop.

And here's the switcheroo:

The coffee shop was where Samantha drove, after closing the store.

There it is again: A convoluted order of events making the head cock to the side and the mind say, "Huh?" The coffee shop is the receiver of Samantha's action (her driving), and by placing the receiver first, we created a passive construction.

Weird. That's right. Complicating a sentence, intentionally or unintentionally, is just plain weird—because we're making life hard on ourselves. Why do we do that, anyway? (*sigh)

Now let's mess up the third sentence, which originally states,

The 39th ISS Progress resupply vehicle automatically docked to the aft port of the Aveda service module of the International Space Station at 7:58 a.m.

Ready...set...MESS:

Off to the aft port of the Aveda service module of the International Space station, the 39th ISS Progress resupply vehicle had been automatically docked.

Admit it: The structure of the sentence makes you want to say, "Come again?"

Notice something about the passive sentences we wrote above: The verb is also in a *to be* form. With a *to be* form, you'll see words like *has been, had been, was, were, could have been,* and so on.

Consider the *to be* verbs your red flags. When writing, avoid the backward *to be* constructions. Notice, I didn't say, *When writing, the verb constructions will have to be what you'll want to avoid.*…That's passive. Simply *avoid passive writing.* Be active.

Can you ever use passive voice? Yes, there are times when passive voice works. If you really don't know who did the action in your sentence, then you could use passive voice in order to avoid using an ambiguous pronoun. (I might have caught you scratching your head. No worries. I'll explain.)

Let's use a sentence about cookies, to make the point. If you don't know who ate the cookie, you might say, "The cookie was eaten by sometime last night" (passive). Or you could simply stick with, "Someone ate the cookie last night" (active).

Cookies aside, did you know that some fancy-schmancy writers often try to use passive writing *on purpose*? Yep. Because scientists and researchers are encouraged to take themselves out of their written work and make the words objective (impartial), scientific writers often use passive voice.

Here's an example: The phrase, "We completed the experiment," uses active voice. But there's another problem with the sentence. The writer used *we* (which is a no-no for their professional field and writing style). So the researcher, trying to get rid of the *we* word thinks that he needs to write, "The experiment was completed" (passive voice). Eek! The poor researchers are stuck in passive mode.

The truth remains: Since we're students and not researchers, active writing is in our best interest—both for effective writing *and* better grades.

Use the active voice.

A final word….
Passive construction: An active style is what you want to write in.

Active construction: Write in an active style.
See the difference?

Active voice is clear, concise, direct, and easily understood. That's why we strive to write in active form.

Write your subject…make the subject immediately act…and you've got it made.

SECTION 3

Paragraphs:
The Core Unit of an Essay or Paper

Chapter 9

Umbrellas, Meat, and PEAs—Oh My!
a.k.a. What Makes a Successful Paragraph?

You now know how to write a solid sentence—one that's not a fragment, not a run on, varies in length, is active (not passive), and clearly states your point. (We've covered a lot of ground already, haven't we?) It's time to move on to the foundational beams of your paper: the paragraph. A paragraph is simply a string of sentences positioned together with direction and purpose.

Paragraphs are single-idea clumps. Every paragraph must be about one thing—and *only* one thing. You pick. Uno idea. A singular focus. Then, once you've decided on that one idea, you have to stick with it. It's true. Once you begin your paragraph, there's no wandering around. It's not allowed.

Now, here's a cool fact. A great paragraph follows specific guidelines. There's a formula, for a well-crafted paragraph. That's right—your paragraph has an instruction manual.

That's good news.

Each paragraph's single idea is divided into three parts: the topic sentence, middle sentences, and the concluding sentence. Sentences within these three parts of the paragraph have jobs—as you say, specific work to do. Once you learn the sentences' jobs, you can put the sentence to work for you. When purpose-driven sentences follow the job they're cut out to do, your paragraphs become clear and make sense to the reader.

Follow me, here. There's hope at the end of the tunnel. This is easy.

Especially with academic writing, the three parts of a paragraph can be organized, or categorized, by their three purposes. The first part is *the point*; the second part is the *evidence*; and the third part is the *analysis*. To remember the three purposes, fondly refer to your paragraph as "eating PEAs" (**p**oint, **e**vidence, **a**nalysis).

Let's go back to the beginning—the point. Every paragraph must have a topic sentence, or the one sentence that tells the reader what the entire paragraph is about. (You may remember this from grade school.)

Topic sentences have guidelines. Guidelines are good. Because when you follow the guidelines, you hit the mark—coming away with a strong, powerful topic sentence (which we want). A strong point. The "P" of "PEAs."

Guideline 1: The topic sentence is a single sentence—and only one.

Guideline 2: The topic sentence is broad. Its purpose and content covers over the whole paragraph.

Guideline 3: The topic sentence loves to come first. In 99 percent of the paragraphs that you'll write, the first sentence of the paragraph will probably be the topic sentence. Can you place the topic sentence somewhere else? Sure, you can. But for academic writing, the topic sentence tends to float to the top of the paragraph, like a cork. Why fight the force of the cork? The top is a safe (and effective) place to be.

Moving on…we're still standing with the topic sentence, the "P" point of your PEAs paragraph, the single, first sentence of your paragraph. Keep your feet planted here, because it's starting to rain.

Let's now refer to the topic sentence as an umbrella because it covers over all of the sentences in your paragraph. Every single paragraph must fall under the "topic" of that sentence—and your topic sentence stretches out and drapes itself over every word beneath it. Every single sentence below the umbrella "attaches back" or relates to the first sentence.

Repeat after me: My topic sentence is broad. My topic sentence is beautiful. My topic sentence is superior. It's superior in its content and its position. And my topic sentence makes a point. The first order of business for any paragraph is always to *make a point*.

By the way, let me tell you a super-amazing secret: The first sentence of each paragraph in your essay or paper clues your professor in on your paper's entire start-to-finish format. With an academic work (or any non-fiction work, for that matter), the reader should be able to find out what your entire paper is about simply by skimming down your page and reading the first line of each paragraph.

In this book's format, you'll notice that each paragraph often begins with the first sentence in bold, a la Internet article style. Bolded first lines make it easy to skim down the page, read the main ideas, and understand the key points quickly. Bolding the first line is a formatting technique popularized by the World Wide Web. For fast reading—and learning—bolding works. By the way, this book's bolded sentences are either topic sentences or "attention grabbers" that lead you to the topic sentence. If you want to, check it out by reading back over just the first lines. It creates a way to get the key ideas, *fast*.

Let's move on.

The middle sentences are the meat of your paragraph sandwich. (The sandwich analogy is the typical word picture given for paragraphs or papers, so you may have heard this before.) What I believe to be most important about the innards of your paragraph is that it's important to put your meat on thick; don't be frugal by placing one skinny slice of info, like a cheap deli sandwich. Be gourmet.

The meaty middle sentences are where the *evidences* of your point are laid out for your reader to chew on. ("Evidence" is the "E" of your PEAs paragraph memory device.) Your meaty evidence middle consists of quotes, facts, and astounding proofs that are going to rock your reader. Such is the job of middle sentences.

On the inside of the paragraph, you'll explain. You'll show examples. You'll tell, in order, why you put that first sentence there, in the first place. You'll provide proof that your first sentence was a good one—that your claim is worthwhile. In an order that makes sense, you'll answer the reader's questions about the first line.

I love this part. I call the paragraph order-of-sentences the "answering questions in a conversation with the reader" part. I love conversations.

Let me show you what I mean. Let's build out a paragraph together—so you can see the cool conversation with the reader in action. And since I'm sitting in a Starbucks while I write this sentence, let's say our opening line (our topic sentence) is this: *Starbucks coffee shops provide multiple options for hot and cold drinks.*

What do you expect the paragraph to be on? Well, we made a claim about many kinds of drinks, so we expect to read about the types of drinks in the paragraph, right? So the first "reader question" is, *what are the different types of drinks I can get at Starbucks?*

Let's answer the reader question. *What are the "multiple options"?* By answering our reader's question, our paragraph now stands as so:

Starbucks coffee shops provide multiple options for hot and cold drinks. Hot drinks are divided into teas, coffees, lattes, and espresso drinks. Cold drinks include frappuccinos, iced coffees, and iced teas. (I'm sure there are more options—after all, it's Starbucks—but for now, let's stop there).

What do we write next? Well, what does the reader want to know?

* If my piece is informational, maybe the reader wants to know what's in those drinks (what they're made of). So we'll describe the contents of the drink (an explanation).
* If my overall essay is about economics and profitability, maybe the reader wants to know how many drinks are sold (facts). I'll quote numbers to prove my point, and tell where I got the quote.
* If I'm writing a research paper, and I'm trying to prove that companies with more product options have a higher volume of sales, I'll quote a source with sales figures proving my point.

Or maybe you want to include all of the above.

Decide what the reader wants to know first, second, and third—and decide if there is any other "proofs" that you can give to the reader, to show them that Starbucks has a fabulous array of options for coffee-shop goers—and what that large array means for you and the company.

Finally, the last sentence of your paragraph is the *analysis*—the "bottom line" of why you put the paragraph in your paper in the first place. Here, as a last wave goodbye to your fabulous paragraph, you'll craftily summarize and draw conclusions for your reader. You'll tell us a take-away point, the synthesis of your ideas, and the so-what of why you put that paragraph in your written piece, in the first place.

Don't leave anything to your reader's imagination. If you quoted Calvin Smith, restate Calvin's key idea and turn that proof into a brick in the solid wall of your argument. We want the reader to be sent off with the most powerful bit of information, causing the entire paragraph to make sense. The goal is for the reader to come away from the paragraph's last line and say, "Yes! Of course!"

Let's wrap up our example paragraph. Why list the options for drinks, anyway? After reading the claim (first sentence) and the explanations and proofs (the inside sentences), analyze what it all means, for Starbucks to have multiple options. Is the final point the idea that just about anyone who visits can find a drink to their liking? Is the analysis more that companies with multiple options get a higher volume of customers? Decide the most important reason for the paragraph, and create a sentence at the end.

Follow the formula for a solid paragraph and your paper starts to write itself. Why? Because a great academic paper is simply a string of great paragraphs. Think of your paper as a stroll through ideas....ideas that are the stepping stones along a path. Better yet, visualize that you're taking the reader on a road trip, hitting all of the hot spots and best restaurants around. With a well-planned itinerary, you'll have an excursion to remember. So plan your stops (your paragraphs) well. Follow the formula. It works.

Chapter 10

Keep Every Paragraph unto Itself
a.k.a. Give Your Paragraph "Strings"

This chapter is short . . . but oh-so important. Because it's often at the paragraph level that your academic work pulls together or falls apart. You may think that paragraph writing is simple. But don't let the seeming-simplicity of writing a short paragraph fool you: Paragraphs can be sneaky, slippery little guys.

Let's imagine that paragraphs are individual persons. Paragraph-persons can be independent and confident or the paragraph-persons can be confused, conflicted, and mixed up with the neighboring paragraphs. It's obvious that we want emotionally-healthy paragraphs: the independent, confident kind. So how do we get our paragraphs healthy?

Our paragraphs have to be single-minded. Single-minded paragraphs aren't influenced by neighboring paragraphs in the least. Single-minded paragraphs hold their own thoughts—not the thoughts of others.

I've said it before: Every single inner sentence of the paragraph—that is, every sentence other than the first and last sentence—has to be congruent with its neighboring sentence. Yes, when it comes to content, the inner sentences have to be completely connected in harmonic theme. The paragraph's thoughts have to be focused and centered, on one, and only one, topic. Seriously, one of the biggest issues with paragraphs is that stray thoughts meander in and plop themselves right down into the middle of it all. How annoying.

Post a sign: No stray thoughts allowed. Your paragraph's inner sentences aren't like reality show contestants trying to be different; your inner sentences are like Whos in Whoville from Dr. Seuss' *How the Grinch Stole Christmas*—holding hands and singing together (I can hear it now…Dah-hoo foor-ays, Dah-hoo door-ays).

Let's go back to our umbrella topic sentence. If your topic sentence is an umbrella, then your middle sentences are the spires within the umbrella, all connected together from the peak down to the pokey umbrella tips. Better yet, imagine that the entire umbrella is your topic sentence—one huge "point" that's arching over your entire paragraph. Now gather up some string and cut pieces off; each string is a sentence. Tie each sentences to the end spires, so that the sentences (strings) are attached to the topic (umbrella). Let the strings hang down, comfortably dangling and swaying in the breeze, forever connected to the over-arching umbrella—and happy to be there. Every sentence "ties back" to the topic sentence perfectly. I admit, it's a silly picture; but it's a picture that you'll remember. Every single sentence has to be connected to the topic, or the sentence doesn't belong.

You have a responsibility to your reader: Before giving your paragraph the head nod to exist in final form, you must examine your inner sentences carefully. Anything that isn't connected must be tossed and forever banished, never to return. If a stray sentence sneaks into your paragraph—making the paragraph slightly schizophrenic—then there's no way on this planet that you're going to convince your reader that you know what you're talking about. You'll lose your flow and maybe even lose your reader. Goodness, that's exactly what we *don't* want to do. With academic writing, this is serious business. You have to convince your reader that you have a firm grasp on the topic at hand. And firm grasps begin within your paragraph's continuity and congruence.

Okay—I absolutely *have* to say something here about getting too attached to our writing. Some of us (maybe even most of us) feel that because we wrote the words on the page, those words are a part of us. The words are an extension of who we are, on the inside, somehow living and breathing, with feelings and everything. The idea of taking out sentences that we've written (especially if we think that the sentence is a beautiful one) is horrifying and unthinkable! That would be so hurtful! The delete key stands on the corner of our keyboard as a hideous enemy to avoid. We think, "I could never take that sentence out! It sounds so good! And I spent so much time writing that fabulous sentence!"

Take a breath. Repeat after me, *again*: *The delete key is my friend.* Yes, you must actually learn to take delight in highlighting that stray sentence, popping your finger onto the delete key, and watching that stray sentence disappear. I mean it. At the risk of sounding callous….If the sentence is a stray thought, the sentence is a stray thought—get over it! Your paper (and professor) will thank you.

So make it a habit: After you write a complete paragraph, double-check the inner sentences' connection to the topic sentence. If the sentence isn't 100% connected, then loose the string and let it fly.

Chapter 11

Step Inside; Don't Leap
a.k.a. Eat a Muffin

Good **paragraphs are linear.** That is, good paragraphs' thoughts travel in a dot-to-dot line. The line of information is straight, smooth, and complete—not lacking in any detail that's needed for clarity and understanding. As an academic writer, our goal is clarity. Our goal is to walk along our paper's content line arm in arm with our reader, who experiences complete understanding. Linear paragraphs give our reader the experience of complete understanding.

Linear writing **is writing that leads from one thought to the next, not leaving anything out.** All of the details needed for absolute comprehension are present. And in order to write linearly, we need to write without assumptions.

Unfortunately, all of us write with assumptions. We assume that the reader has prior knowledge. But if you ever took a personal communications course, you know that assuming isn't good. When you assume that your reader knows something—and he or she *doesn't*—then your reader won't follow your point. You lose your reader. The grasp on the reader's arm loosens, and our locked-elbows connection with the reader become barely-touching arms. We drift away from each other.

The result: The reader feels disconnected, becomes confused, and loses interest.

Don't you wish that you could squeeze your thoughts across time and space directly into your reader's mind? I sure do. Too bad that our reader can't Vulcan Mind Meld with us like in Star Trek (go Spock). No, we have to use specific words in a specific order to get across specific ideas...not leaving anything out.

How good are you at writing linearly? In the classroom, I like to ask my students to write a simple, single paragraph called, "How to Eat a Muffin." Here's how it works: Imagine that an alien wants to eat a muffin but doesn't know how (because it never saw a muffin before). The students' job is to write instructions regarding how to eat the muffin. Sounds simple, right? It's not. To prove the point, I become the alien—and after the students write their muffin-eating instructions, I follow what the students wrote. Exactly.

The results are predictable. No matter the student's age (high school freshman to a college master's student), the first thing that the students usually write is, "Pick up the muffin." So I grab the muffin with both hands from the top, like a crane descending on a mound of dirt. The results are rather crumbly. Students realize quickly that writing "pick up the muffin" is full of assumptions. The students assumed that the alien knew which side is up. Students also assumed that the alien knows to wrap its fingers around the sides of the muffin.

Good writers don't assume that the reader holds prior knowledge. Students writing for the alien have to describe which side is up. Students have to describe how the alien will carefully wrap its digits around the paper encasement, and then raise the muffin off of the surface where it presently sits. Eating a muffin becomes an intricate writing exercise.

How does writing about eating a muffin transfer into writing an argumentative paper in high school or college? I'm glad that you asked.

In an argumentative paper, your goal is to delineate information and lay out proofs to convince your reader to side with you on a topic. First, you must describe the present situation. Describing takes linear writing—clearly laying out information to explain, illustrate, and elucidate the topic to the reader. Next, you must prove. Proving takes linear writing—clearly demonstrating, verifying, and establishing a position. In both describing and proving, you may not write with assumptions. Again, assumptions lose the reader. Especially in academic writing, losing the reader is a cardinal sin. So, in academic essays and papers, *muffin writing* becomes a necessity: making no assumptions, leaving nothing out.

Linear writing is also like using stepping stones across a river. Growing up, I remember visiting Milham Park in Kalamazoo, Michigan (yes, there really is a Kalamazoo). A stream winds through the middle of Milham Park, and there is a point along the stream where there's a little island. At one specific place where the water is shallow, people can get to the island by walking across a half-dozen-or-so stones that someone placed in steps from one side to the other. Of course, as kids, we tried to jump over some of the stones instead of stepping. We always ended up wet. Jumping didn't get us there (at least, it didn't get us there *dry*).

Jumping doesn't work in academic writing, either. We have to step on each and every point, each and every idea, and each and every detail that is pertinent to our reader's understanding.

So when you're inside your paragraph, step—don't leap. Take the reader's perspective, so that you can give the reader the exact details that he or she needs for complete comprehension. Then your paragraph will be easy to follow, easy to understand—and, hopefully, easy to agree with.

Chapter 12

Leave Hansel and Gretel Trails
a.k.a. Answer, "What's next?"

Linear sentences within paragraphs have many jobs. We've learned that one job is to be connected to the topic sentence. A second job is to wrap the paragraph in purpose, make a point, show evidence, and give analysis. Yet another job is to step from one sentence to the next, in a linear fashion. The fourth job for our sentences is to know the reader's mind and the future. You heard me right: Your job, as a writer, is to be a sage—perceptive, clever, wise, and astute as to what the reader is going to think of next.

"Oh, now you're saying that we need to be mind readers!" That's right. The best writers know what the reader will think next: what thoughts your reader will mull over, what ideas the reader will be led to, and what questions the reader will ponder—as a result of the sentence that you wrote a second ago. The best writers put themselves in the reader's mind and write as if approaching the material from a place of innocence and naiveté. Only when you write from that pure place will you truly write as if you're inside your reader's mind.

Each sentence that you write spurs a thought. Thoughts have to be addressed with subsequent sentences. Sentences act as Hansel and Gretel trails—as pieces of bread, leading your reader down the path to home. Only by making trails will you fully please your reader—because you've given the reader exactly what he or she needs, to follow your thoughts.

Here's how it works: If you write, "In *King Arthur: Dark Age Warrior and Mythic Hero,* author John Matthews states that, after the battle in AD 501, the end of the Arthur story appears to exist in few surviving historical documents." So what is the reader's next thought? That's easy: *What are the surviving historical documents?* There. You did it. You read the reader's mind. Now go and write what the reader expects next.

With every academic work that you write, you simply have to practice mind reading. Come to think of it, the mind-reading, trail-leaving stuff works for *all* writing. So whether you're writing an essay, a paper, an email, a letter, a memo, a report, or a website text—write through mind reading.

Let's test your sagacious-ability. Here's a sentence; tell me what comes next (this one's simple): "Maple trees develops schizocarps." So what's the reader's question? *What are schizocarps?* You'd better believe that your next sentence will define schizocarps. By the way, schizocarps are the two-sided, wind-dispersed winged fruits that fly off maple trees, also called samaras. When we were little, some of us called the crispy brown structures *helicopters.* (I thought I'd better let you know now, so that you don't wonder all day.)

Now for a harder one; here's your sentence: "The magnetosphere protects the earth from dangerous particles from the sun." What do you think that the reader will ask next? Will it be, *why does the sun have dangerous particles?* Or will the reader's question be, *why does the earth need protecting from particles? What will the particles do?* All three questions are valid. So you'll have to answer all three questions. Decide which question is the burning question, or the logical next step, and then begin writing. (As for the particles, I don't know what they are. You'll have to look that one up yourself, because this paragraph's getting too long.)

One last hint on how to develop trail-writing: Don't write from the position of standing on the trail. It's too close a view to see where you're going (the old, *you can't see the forest for the trees* phenomenon). Practice the *airplane view.* An airplane view is obviously a view from above—seeing the layout of the streets, the town, and the countryside. It's a map view. It's a Global Positioning System (GPS) view. Look down onto your page as from an airplane, a map, or a GPS view, to get a general feel for where you're going. Ask yourself, "what is the overall idea that I want to get across?" Then come up with a step-by-step logical presentation.

Put yourself within the reader's mind, answer the reader's logical questions, and lay out the bread crumbs for the reader to follow. *But I thought you said to write within the reader's mind!* You can think of the reader's next question while in the airplane view. Both perspectives make you an effective writer.

So, when it comes to writing excellent sentences within your paragraph, you now have yet one more thing to think about. No worries. Our great-sentence-writing parts and pieces get easier as you use them. The more that you write and practice the ideas presented in each chapter, the more the ideas make sense. Connect well-structured sentences into a path, and lead your reader along. Answer your reader's questions as you go. Write from a place within your reader's mind.

In many ways, your mantra is, *be the reader*. Satisfy what your reader wants to know next, and your reader will follow you anywhere.

Chapter 13

Give me Closure, Please!
a.k.a. Wrap it Around or Send 'em Off

It's time to give our paragraph closure. We've presented a topic sentence and our *point*. We've written connected, linear, supportive *evidence* sentences. And now it's time to say "so long" to our paragraph. We can say goodbye one of two ways: 1) State the "so what" *analysis* or 2) throw the reader into a new idea. Both ways have reasons why you'd use that specific technique for closure. Both ways work. Let's look at the two ways to close the door on your paragraph.

The "so what" analysis is a *conclusion*. Conclusions give us bottom lines. Conclusions are finale songs that have no curtain call; when it's finished, it's finished—and the audience (the reader) feels good inside, because the part of the topic that we're discussing is exhausted and the questions are answered. You've wrapped up the main point with a scrutiny and examination that leaves the reader with a sense of, "So *that's* what it's all about. I get it." The definition of *conclusion* is to end, to terminate, to finish your thought.

Sometimes the last sentence of a paragraph is a conclusion/analysis statement. Conclusion/analysis statements wrap up a paragraph quite nicely. We take all of the information that we've just shared and put it into a *so-there-you-have-it* ending sentence. I use a conclusion statement at the end of the paragraph above this one. Check it out now.

Academic writing can also use what's called a "send off" sentence. An example of a send off sentence can be found in the first paragraph of this chapter, which states, "Let's look at the two ways to close the door on your paragraph." That sentence is no conclusion at all; I'm sending you off into the next paragraph with an expectation. I've told you, "Heads up! Here comes something new." Now, in an academic paper, understand that you'd never speak directly to the reader as I am within this book. In academia, the technique is a bit trickier to accomplish. I'll show you two ways to send off your reader. (There—I did it again. That last sentence was a send off sentence.)

In academic writing, send off sentences can be *hints* or *shouts*. A *hint* is also known as a *plant*...no, not planting a bomb...planting an *idea* through a

EB Conroy, MA, MFA

single word. The single word gives the reader a clue as to what's coming in the next paragraph. A *shout,* on the other hand, is exactly that—an exclamation that says, "Yo! Here it is!" Again, both send-offs are effective, depending on your content and your purpose.

Here's an example of a paragraph that ends with both a conclusion *and* the hint version of a send off sentence:

> According to James W. Matheson, author of the book *Green Technology,* an example of "technology meeting nature" exists in a facility called the Michigan Technical Education Center (M-TEC).[2] The M-TEC building is located in The Groves, a business, education, and technology park within a local community college's facilities. Surrounded by a park-like setting, M-TEC houses conferences, seminars, training, and business meetings. The focus of M-TEC is presenting state-of-the-art accommodations within relaxed surroundings. Blending function with nature, M-TEC is one of thousands of facilities emerging within the last ten years whose purpose is to create a new breed of "green services and facilities"[3] to a globally-sensitive generation.
>
> "The 'green' trend can be found everywhere," states Marilyn Crawford, PhD. "Our research shows that the percentage of Americans who 'think green' is increasing by multiple percentage points each year."[4] (and so on…)

In the example above, did you follow the *hint* at the end of the first paragraph? The last sentence in the first paragraph not only made an analysis statement that "thousands of facilities have emerged," but the sentence also hinted toward a discussion of "green" in the next paragraph (a global trend). "Green services" moves into "green trend." What a smooth move, eh? By

---

[2] This is a fake footnote, to show you what a real footnote would look like on the bottom of the page. Each number that's placed in the text has a matching footnote number (and what's called *entry*) below—in this space. The info here tells you where you got the quoted material. Sometimes the footnotes tell you a special tidbit (a by-the-way comment) about what's in the text. But I'm getting ahead of myself…

[3] This is another fake footnote. FYI, anything in quotation marks has to have a little footnote number next to it, just like this one. Really. It's a rule. You have to tell the reader where you got the quoted material. To find out more about how to do this kind of cool footnoting, get *Simplified Research Writing*—the book that follows this one. It's stuff you'll need to know.

[4] Ta-da! Here's where you'd place the reference for Marilyn Crawford's quote.

using similar words (and thoughts), the last sentence sent the reader off into the next topic quite nicely.

With the same basic paragraph, let's look at an example of a send off that's a *shout*. I've changed the text a little bit. See if you can pick up the difference:

> According to James W. Matheson, author of the book *Green Technology*, an example of "technology meeting nature"[5] exists in a facility called the Michigan Technical Education Center (M-TEC). The M-TEC building is located in The Groves, a business, education, and technology park within a local community college's facilities. Surrounded by a park-like setting, M-TEC houses conferences, seminars, training, and business meetings. The focus of M-TEC is presenting state-of-the-art accommodations within relaxed surroundings. Blending function with nature, M-TEC is one of thousands of facilities emerging within the last ten years whose purpose is to create a new breed of "green services and facilities."[6] According to Matheson, today's globally-sensitive generation is more than an idea; it's a trend.[7]
>
> "The 'green' trend can be found everywhere," states Marilyn Crawford, PhD. "Our research shows that the percentage of Americans who 'think green' is increasing by multiple percentage points each year." (and so on...)

The *shout* sends the reader directly into the next paragraph. Here's how: The first paragraph's last sentence directly correlates with the words in the next paragraphs first sentence. Sound confusing? It's not really.

Take a look at (and analyze) the second example again. The words

---

[5] Woo-hoo! Here we go again! Something is quoted, so you have to put a footnote next to it. If you were using a *parenthetical reference style,* your info would be between parentheses, and you'd have a page at the end, with the where-you-got-it info. Again, get *Simplified Research Writing,* to know the difference.

[6] One more time! Here's the footnote entry for the little number 5 in the example above. If this was a real footnote, then you'd find information here on the *source* from whence the information came (the book, article, newspaper, DVD, or even personal interview...however and wherever you got the info).

[7] And finally, here's the last footnote space that, since my example up above is simply made up, has no real source to put here. But you have to admit, it looks cool.

repeat and blend. This particular *shout* version is a transition; transitions repeat and blend. In the next chapter, we'll talk about transitions and *tail-to-head* connections. But for now, simply focus on the idea of wrap-ups and send-offs; know that your last sentence can be a door completely closed...or a door swung open. You can use either.

Here's one last thing to remember: While topic sentences are often global in their content, conclusion statements are often specific. Did you get that? Topic sentence = broad. Last sentence = specific.

No matter if your last sentence is a wrap-around or send-off, you'll want to funnel your words down to key ideas. Leave your reader with the best notion—something to consider...a strong impression, a key inspiration, a specific proposal, or a unique view. Even with what you might consider a little paragraph, with a small amount of information, end well.

Well-written little paragraphs make well-written essays, well-written compositions, and well-written research papers.

True story.

Chapter 14

Connect and Transition
a.k.a. Chase Your Tail

There's a trick to making writing flow. No doubt, you and I understand that not all writing flows. We've all faced writing that skitters, skips, and jumps from idea to idea. When attempting to read writing with skitters, we read the paragraph over and over, trying to figure out what in the world the writer's saying. Two words come to mind, for non-connected writing: The first is *yuck* (that's an unofficial but extremely apropos word, if I do say so myself) and the second is *frustrating* (that's the official word). As we've already discussed, you can make your writing flow by writing in a linear fashion. But there are also special words that help the reader to move smoothly through our writing.

We're talking about *connectives* and *transitions*. Connectives and transitions are words or phrases that help you (and the reader) organize ideas. Connectives and transitions show the relationship between ideas. And they help the reader understand how your ideas mesh.

I believe that connectives are slightly different from transitions. A *connective* makes the *inside* of the paragraph flow. Connectives make your paragraph's middle sentences affectionately hold hands. *Transition* words love to nudge the reader, moving the reader forward with a push to the next sentence. Transitions are also fond of residing at the ends and beginnings of paragraphs, as opposed to hanging out within paragraph's middle (like a connective).

Let's talk about connectives first.

Connectives are words that attach, tie, join, and bond your ideas together. Connectives hook up your ideas like those little magnetic buttons on a child's train set. If you didn't have one of those while growing up, then I insist that you go to the children's section at a Barnes and Noble store and look for the train table. There, you'll find a magnetic-attachment toy train cars. Go ahead: Play with the cars. Tell the store associate that your writing teacher told you to do it. And while you're at it, strike up a conversation about connectives. It could be fun.

Here is a list of common connectives—including what the connectives do and which are appropriate to use. I've separated out the connectives into the categories of what they're for—their job, in your writing. Under each job, you'll find a category: academic, mid-range, and non-academic. These are my groupings—subgroups, if you will—that help you to know which words are most typically used for each audience (from super informal and chummy, right on up to the highest black-suit-and-tie formal audience). Take a peek now at the words that you can use to make your writing flow.

Example or illustration

Academic: For example; specifically; to illustrate; another case is found in
Mid-range academic use: for instance; in particular; a case in point may be
Non-academic: particularly; to be specific; by way of illustration (conversational and more relaxed)

Emphasis

Academic: further, furthermore; moreover; yet again
Mid-range academic use: in particular; even more so, even more; above all, most of all; how much more
Non-academic (unless used in a quote from an expert or reliable source, because the words insinuate superiority and author opinion): In fact; indeed; without a doubt; undoubtedly; surely; to be sure; truly; certainly; I am certain; besides; add to this (Writer beware! The phrase uses *this,* a word on the No-No List...see Chapter 1.)

Comparison

Academic: similarly; likewise; in like manner/in a like manner; parallel with; comparable to, a comparable view is; from another perspective; in like manner; a similar view is that; in contrast; conversely
Mid-range academic use: in the same way; from another point of view; in the same category; yet more important may be X, of less importance may be X (a phrase that's leaning toward personal opinion, unless supported by evidence...so be careful, using this one)
Non-academic: just as/just like (uses *just*—a word to avoid from The List in Chapter 1); in contrast with this (uses *this*)

Exceptions

Academic: with the exception of; excluding/excluded
Mid-range academic use: exclusive of (syntax may become awkward with the *of* position)
Non-academic: with this exception, except for this, this exception made, leaving out this exception, excluding this point (all use *this*...so avoid, in academic writing)

Explaining

No real academic uses. Usually, there's no need to say that you're explaining. Simply move to the point and explain away.

Mid-range academic use: in other words, which amounts to (leaning toward conversational)

Non-academic: to explain (telling the reader what you're doing); this is to say (uses *this*); that is (a use much like *this* and conversational)

Purpose and returning to purpose

Academic: In order to X (X being the desired result from the upcoming action); then

Mid-range academic uses: once more; as stated (moving toward conversationally talking to the reader)

Non-academic: for this purpose; so that this purpose occurs (obviously uses *this*—eek! Read chapter one again, if you don't get why I'm screeching at the thought.); as I've said (avoid personal pronoun and contractions); to continue, to return, to resume, along with (telling the reader what you're doing...a no-no); at any rate, at all events, in any event (colloquial)

Returning to a point or idea

Academic: with respect to; in relation to/as related to

Midrange academic uses: concerning

Non-academic: as for

To acknowledge or admit a point

Academic: although, even though, while true in specific cases, while it is true

Mid-range academic use: granted (the word is more conversational; therefore, its status goes down on the academic scale)

Non-academic: while this is true; while this may or may not be true (uses *this*)

Making conclusions, connections, and judgments

Academic: therefore; consequently; as a result;

Midrange academic uses: thus, hence (older English); for the reason of X; if X is true, then; in the case of X; under the circumstance of X

Non-academic: because of this, for this reason, this being true, in this case, as this is the case, under this circumstance, under these circumstances (use *this* and *these*); what follows is

There are quite a few connective words, aren't there? That's good news for you. You can pick and choose the right word, to make your entire paragraph flow like melted chocolate over your favorite dessert. But don't let the chocolaty word picture fool you. Chocolaty connective words make chocolaty, smooth paragraphs...but the words, themselves, are power-packed

EB Conroy, MA, MFA

sweet things that stir the chocolate with gusto and propel the reader.

Transition words are a bit different than connectives: they shift, change, and move your ideas forward. They can be pushy. Oh, they're not loud-mouthed or overassertive. They're more like your friend who knows what's best for you—making a link from one idea to the next, much like your friend hooking you up with the guy or gal you always wanted to talk with. Transitions bring next-step logical movement to your sentences. It's good.

Here is a list of common transitions—what they do and which are appropriate to use:

Cause and effect
Academic: therefore, since; consequently; as a result
Mid-range academic use: Because; thus, hence, thereby, thereto, thereof, therein (more old-English style transitions…so not as common and may not be appropriate); in such cases/in such a case, at such times, on such occasions (*such* is close to *this*)
Non-academic: because of this, in this case, together with this, in all this, in connection with this, in addition to this, under these circumstances (uses *this, these*); here again (conversational)

Conceding
None of the conceding transitions are appropriate for academic use, as the words give author opinion and talk to the reader: Certainly; indeed; I admit, admittedly; true, it is true; granted; no doubt, doubtless; to be sure

Contrast
Academic: however; nevertheless; despite; in spite of
Mid-range academic use: on the contrary (leaning toward colloquial)
Non-academic: still; on the other hand (colloquial)

Denoting time
Academic: next; previously; immediately; eventually; gradually; then; before/after, afterward; earlier/later; finally; often; formerly, at an earlier time/period, throughout the period, during the period of X, throughout the period of X; at the same moment; in the end; at length
Mid-range academic use: soon
Non-academic: now, now that; meanwhile, in the meantime; suddenly; then (tend to be used in conversational writing), since then; by that time; at last; henceforth, thereafter (antiquated); to begin with

Denoting space
Academic: beside; in front of; behind; next to; beyond; above; below; inside; outside; across; opposite; surrounding; to the right/left; to the side of
Mid-range academic use: near; far; around
Non-academic: near to/nearly; far from; opposite to; outside of/inside of; alongside; there

Adding to
Academic: in addition; also; another; furthermore; moreover; first/second/third/etc.; perhaps equally important
Mid-range academic use: too
Non-academic: and then

To note a change in your point
Academic: in general
Mid-range academic use: in another case, in other cases
Non-academic: at the least/at least; seriously, in seriousness, in all seriousness; joking aside, jesting aside; to speak frankly; to get to the point, to come to the point; of course; you see; as it stands; in another way (all conversational); in my mind (uses the personal pronoun *my*)

Opposing and refuting
Academic: Yet; nevertheless, none the less; otherwise; however; even so; despite X; if X were not so, then; contrary to X; though X
Mid-range academic use: at the same time, on the other hand; on the contrary; only
Non-academic: in spite of this, was this not so (uses *this*); the fact is, despite the fact that; after all (colloquial and tells the reader)

To summarize
Academic: A summary of X shows; the logical conclusion, as shown by X, is; the conclusion is; finally; briefly
Mid-range academic use: In summary; to summarize; in conclusion, to conclude (each shows tells the reader what you're doing and, as such, lowers its status on the academic writing word choice scale)
Non-academic: in short; all-in-all, last of all; in other words, in a word, in short (conversational); to sum up (telling the reader what you're doing); as we have seen, as we have concluded, as we have understood, I hope I have made it clear (uses the personal pronoun *we* and talks to the reader); up to this point (uses *this* and is conversational); yes, no (talking to the reader); lastly (it's simply awkward)

Okay—on to the last point of the chapter.

EB Conroy, MA, MFA

There's one more trick to making your writing flow. It has to do with what I call *connectors* (not connec*tives*, mind you…connec*tors*). Connectors are ways to arrange your words and phrases to increase the forward motion of (and coherence within) your writing. I'm quite fond of two connectors.

The first connector that I'm quite fond of is using an amazingly-cool trick called *tail to head construction.* A tail to head construction has to do with taking words (or phrases) at the end of a paragraph and repeating the words at the beginning of the next paragraph. If you look closely, you'll find that I used tail to head connector in this paragraph. Go back and look for the phrase, "I'm quite fond of." That's my connector. It makes the last paragraph flow into this one.

Why is the technique called *tail to head*? The word picture is of a dog chasing its tail—which I think is pretty hilarious (and helps me to remember the technique). A dog chases its tail in a continuous movement—with no start and stop, no beginning and end. Your paper can flow with no start and stop, smoothly from beginning to end, when you use the tail to head connector.

Here's how to use tail to head: Simply choose a key word or phrase and weave it into the last sentence of the paragraph and the first sentence of the next paragraph. It's not hard to do. I did it again in this paragraph and the previous. Look back. You'll see the words *tail to head* in the last sentence and then again in my opening line. You see how simple it is, to put the technique into action? Tail to head is a low-effort endeavor.

When using tail to head, there is one caution to keep in mind, though. You mustn't use too strong a connection. If you copy the words too closely, your connector may feel stilted and juvenile. So it does take a bit of practice, to make the tail to head seamless.

The last connector is related to tail to head. It's simply *repetition*. Repetition within the paragraph causes flow and cohesion, much like an interior decorator repeating a color, pattern, or theme to create flow and cohesion to the ambiance of a room.

Repetition can come in the form of a single word or a phrase; repetition can also come in the form of parallel structure. In my home, I have a plant thing going. Aside from real plants hanging here or there, I have paintings with leaves and petals hanging on the walls. I also have green accents around the room—like the green blanket tossed over the edge of the chair. To create theme, I've used repetition of object and color. The effect is a cohesion that, when I sit on the couch and type this chapter, feels great to me. You can make your paragraphs feel great (and have flow) by using repetition.

Here's an example paragraph, from one of my upcoming fiction books, *The Write Deception*, which uses repetition:

> She loved the newness—the new job, the new corner cafes, the new people…even her new habit of greeting the cute little old bald man at the corner flower shop who always talked about his wife, *God rest her blessed soul*, and his son, *the artist who has dreams without bottoms on them*. She loved the way he always gave her an extra bud, *to anticipate a beautiful new tomorrow*. How did he know that she needed those exact words?

Did you catch the repetitive word that gave the paragraph cohesion and flow? The word is *new*. What's really fun about using the word *new* is that the entire theme of the book is about taking chances and experiencing life anew. Using repetition as a connector—and more—is absolutely fun, isn't it?

Finally, here's an academic example of repetition from a seminary student's paper. Students of all ages call, asking for help, and the author of this 30-page final paper was wallowing in run-on sentences. We needed to clean up the writing, to make it more direct, in order to match the style of academic writing that the instructor expected. In the *literature review* section of the student's work, repetition was one of the tricks that she ended up using, for cohesion. Check it out.

> God's many names define His character. God is Triune, also called "three in One," as the Father, Son and Holy Spirit. God is Eternal, having no beginning and no end (Psalm 90:2). God is also called all powerful, almighty, and omnipotent (Job 42:2, Matthew 19:26). God is omniscient and all knowing (Psalm 139:2-4); He is omnipresent or "everywhere present (Psalm 139:7-10, Ephesians 4:6). And
>
> God is Holy, meaning He is complete, whole, pure, and sinless (Deuteronomy 32:4, Psalm 92:15). The characteristics of God point to salvation, and God's attributes explain humankind's need for salvation.

While the paragraph is straightforward and arguably plain, a word and phrase pops out to create cohesion. The word *God* and phrase *God is* creates a clean flow to the paragraph. Flow is always good. Flow is our goal. Flow is what makes your reader read effortlessly. Flow makes your reader feel surprise, when he or she arrives at the end of the paper, and the feeling is, "Oh! I'm here already. That was fast." And perhaps most importantly, flow helps your reader feel good about what you've written.

EB Conroy, MA, MFA

So don't go with the jump; go with the flow. Use connectives, transitions, and connectors.

SECTION 4

Punctuation:
Cutting Comma Chaos

Chapter 15

Know Your No-Comma Addition
a.k.a. This and That Needs No Comma

Commas create chaos. Seriously. Through the years of teaching writing at two different higher institutions of learning, comma errors continue to be the blight of oh-so-many of my students' papers. It's sad. Nobody seems to know what to do with the poor little things; comma intelligence appears to be mislaid. Commas are either completely left out in the cold (rarely or never to appear on the page) or they're so splattered on the sheet in a wild population explosion that the average person can't turn this way or that without bumping shoulders with yet one more dropped-down curly-cue.

We're going to set commas straight once and for all. With simplicity. In this section of the book, we'll confer together regarding what I believe to be the four most-common comma errors and then give straightforward solutions to each. Then, with understanding in hand, all you have to do is follow the solutions.

I warn you: We are *not*, I repeat *not*, going to have an English lesson. We won't even use words like "dependent clause" and "comma splice." We *are* going to simplify comma usage into its most basic elements, using everyday street language (the clean kind). I call it *functional learning*: the focus is on function, not nomenclature. The result should be the ability to use the silly things correctly, once and for all.

Here we go.

The first correct comma usage solution uses simple addition.
Mathematical addition uses numbers: *one plus one*. No-comma addition uses words or phrases: *word-or-phrase plus word-or-phrase*.

But we don't use a plus sign. In our no-comma addition for using commas correctly, the *plus sign* in the equation we're going to use is substituted with a word from this list: ***and, but, or, for, nor, so,*** and ***yet***.

Those little connecting words that unite ideas and sentences are called conjunctions. (Okay, I lied; we *are* using some official English-class words. But that's only because I know that you can handle it. Back to no-comma addition....)

These little itty-bitty add-together conjunction words' job is to connect—and absolutely NO COMMAS ARE INVOLVED in our addition, at all, forever and ever, Amen.

Hear me on this again: *No-comma addition does not use commas.*

This is what it looks like:

Word-or-phrase CONJUNCTION word-or-phrase

*dogs **and** cats...*
*not here **but** there...*
*wooden **or** granite table tops...*
*was unbelievable **for** George's understanding...*
*neither here **nor** there...*
*arriving early **so** we wouldn't miss the show...*
*she was happy **yet** overwhelmed...*

As you can figure out in the examples above, combining words with No Comma Addition happens all kinds of ways. Don't panic. Let's start with how it works with single words. (Simple.)

We can create addition by combining *a single word with a single word*. Here's an example: "Marcus Hollingsworth wrote <u>monographs **and** journal articles</u>." Pretty simple, eh?

It's easy to see if we need a comma or not. To check for no-comma addition, we drop out the two things that are added together, and put in "this and that" in its place. In the example above, we say, "Marcus Hollingsworth wrote this and that" (Hey—you're getting the hang of this.)

See? It works. Monographs and journals....two items...we have a *this and that* connection, so don't put a comma there, because no comma needed. No-comma addition means you leave the commas out. Yes, I'm repeating myself. This and that. Leave commas out.

We can connect with the little word *or*, too: "Marcus Hollingsworth wrote **either** monographs **or** journal articles." Note that when we used the word *or*, we had to add the word *either*. They're a matched pair, traveling together. Always use one with the other. And, of course, using *either-or* changes the meaning of the sentence, doesn't it?

We also create no-comma addition by combining *a phrase with a phrase*. Here's an example: "The summary can **either** capture the essence of the author's idea **or** quote the author directly; both devices are effective." With no-comma addition, the sentence states, "The summary can either do this or that; both devices are effective." We used the no-comma addition principle again...so we don't need a comma. The sentence passed the test, to leave the comma out.

You're doing so well, let's make the example sentences just a tiny bit trickier.

We can also create no-comma addition by combining a long phrase with an equally-long phrase. Connecting extra-long phrases takes a little bit of figuring, but if we're on our guard, we can still spy the *no-comma addition* factor and keep the comma out.

Here's our example sentence: "Simply label the item to the left of the conjunction 'this' and label the item to the right of the conjunction 'that.'" By underlining the two long pieces, and finding the "and" in the middle, *ta-da*— we easily figure out that we have a *this and that* construction...so we keep the comma out.

Danger: When adding long phrases together in a sentence, you and I both know that everybody and their dog wants to throw in two or three extra commas, for supposed-clarity. Stay strong. Resist the urge. Resisting placing commas where they (technically) don't belong serves you well, in the end.

Okay, one more thing.

Here's a confusing "this and that" addition problem: Equally weighted *complete sentences* (not phrases) also become "this and that" constructions, where we leave the comma out. No lie.

For instance, check this sentence out: "The manufacturer continued to place the blame on the consumer **and** the consumer continued to place the blame on the manufacturer." Yes, there are two compete sentences on either side of the word, "and." But the whole thing is a "this and that." Really.

The key is that both sides of the "and" (even though they're complete sentences) are *equally weighted*. The second sentence on the right side of the "and" does not move the reader forward; the two sentences are simply adding two thoughts together. Chew on that idea for a while. Complete-sentence "this and that" constructions are sometimes the trickiest to grasp.

Just remember this: If you have complete sentences on either side of your "and" (or "but," or any other conjunction), and you can easily switch the sentences around (either sentence can go first), *then you don't have to use a comma before the conjunction.* (Wow.)

When no-comma addition gets complicated, professional writers do one of two things: Either call your editor (to find out what to do) or change the sentence construction (to avoid the issue). Seriously. That's what professionals do.

Even professional writers bicker and blubber over where commas go. For published works such as books, magazine articles, and journal articles, an editor steps in as the final word regarding where to place commas. And editors are all different; they have preferences. At that point, writers rarely argue with the editor; we bow to the editors' preference.

You say you don't write articles for publication and don't have an editor? Silly me—I forgot. If you have no editor and you're confused regarding the comma, then 1) ask the instructor what he/she prefers or 2) try changing your sentence construction. Yep. It's not running away. It's *being creative.* You've heard it said, *there's more than one way to skin a cat* (I always thought that was an awful visual image…)? Well, with writing, there's more than one way to arrange a group of words. Rewrite. I'm not joking. There's no shame in rewriting.

So here's your solution to questions regarding no-comma addition: If you can substitute the words, *this and that* into your sentence (or *either this or that*…or *neither this nor that* … or *this but that*…or *this yet that* … I know, you get it), then you have *no-comma addition*—and no comma is needed. Leave the curly-cues out. You'll need the little guys for your clauses, complete sentences, and lists…which lead us to the next chapters. Read on….

Chapter 16

Comma-off Your Clauses
a.k.a. By the way,

Not all commas are hard to understand; commas with clausettes are fairly easy to spot. What's a clausette? No, we're not talking about a female Santas dropping off presents on Christmas Eve. We're talking about a word I made up.

Yep. I made up a word. Don't shoot me.

Clausette Definition: [noun] An extra *piece* of a sentence—a single word or longer part—that adds extra information, to clarify or spice up the main sentence. A clausette is *by the way* information that adds to your sentence's main idea, as if someone is whispering to the side, "Oh, and, by the way, you might want to know *this* little bit of info, too."

Clausettes *add something special*—something more—to the basic, complete sentence.

The phrase, "By the way," is a clausette—a fragment, a piece—in and of itself. That's why *by the way* is such a great way to remember how the clausette thing works. If you can identify *by the way* extra information in your sentence—the parts that are aside from your *main* sentence—then you have a clausette on your hands.

And the clausette shows you where to put your comma. Pure and simple.

It's time to examine your sentences. Because you need to find the "main" or "real" sentence, and then find the "by the way" "clausette"…because POOF—with the main sentence and the "by the way" piece identified, you'll finally know how to solve some of the hardest where-to-put-the-comma struggles.

Here's how it works: The *by the way* info absolutely has to be set apart from the main sentence with a comma (or commas, plural, if the *by the way* extra piece is stuck in the middle of the sentence).

What great news! We can now clear up comma placement with clausettes, simply and quickly.

Follow this three-step formula.

Step number one: Find the main sentence.
Step number two: Find the extra, whispered-to-the-side, *by the way* info.
Step number three: Place a comma (or commas) between the two.

One, two, three—comma confusion conquered! Seriously. That's it. (You can stop sweating bullets now.)

Let's try out the three-step solution with some real-life sentences. The following sentences are missing their *by the way* commas. Let's put them in.

Example 1
"According to James P. Curry the Smithsonian's collection is the most complete collection available today."

- Number one, find the main sentence: The main sentence is, "The Smithsonian's collection is the most complete collection available today."

- Number two, find the extra, whispered-to-the-side *by the way* info: The clausette is, "According to James P. Curry." The main sentence can stand alone, without the clausette; that's how we know that "according to James P. Curry" is a clausette.

- And finally, Number three: Place a comma between the two. "According to James P. Curry, the Smithsonian's collection is the most complete collection available today."

  Ta-da. Clause found, comma placed, sentence complete. Oh. So. Easy.

  Example 1 is called the *beginning clausette* because the clause is placed at the beginning of the sentence. Basic. Simple. Not hard to find. Straightforward. And used quite a bit in academic writing.

Example 2
"Clothing companies although typically thrilled by economic upturns are increasingly concerned."

- **Number one, find the main sentence:** "Clothing companies are increasingly concerned."

  (Ooh, that sentence is cut into two pieces, isn't it? Thought I'd trick you, but you're too smart.)

- **Number two, find the "by the way" clause (extra info):** "although typically thrilled by economic upturns."

  ("Although" is a trigger word...remember that, if you will.)

- **Number three, add the commas:** "Clothing companies, although typically thrilled by economic upturns, are increasingly concerned." Ta-da again—and again! Clausette found, two commas placed. Since the *by the way* clausette interrupts the main sentence, falling smack-dab into the middle of it all, then we simply place commas on both sides of the *by the way* clausette.

  Example 2 is called a *middle clausette* because the clause is placed in the middle of the sentence. Easy. Uncomplicated. Direct. Accomplishable. And used a fair amount in academic writing.

Example 3
"Corporate leaders believe that specialty programs will eventually fulfill the federal government's expectations particularly if state governments fulfill their promises for fund distribution."

- **Number one, find the main sentence:** "Corporate leaders believe that specialty programs will eventually fulfill the federal government's expectations."

  (We've got some longer sentences traipsing around, don't we? No worries. You can do this.)

- **Number two, find the *by the way* clausette:** "particularly if state governments fulfill their promises for fund distribution."

  ("Particularly if" is a trigger phrase...it has "if," and "if" is a "by the way" word.)

- **Number three, add the comma:** "Corporate leaders believe that specialty programs will eventually fulfill the federal government's

EB Conroy, MA, MFA

expectations, particularly if state governments fulfill their promises for fund distribution."

The third example is called an *end clausette* because the *by the way* is placed at the end of the sentence. Example 3 was a bit more complicated because the sentence was longer, with more information; but the process of finding where to place the comma was the same. It's predictable. Workable. As easy as one-two-three.

End clausettes aren't used as much in academic writing, because the end clausette tends to leave the reader with the aside (the non-essential info), as opposed to the key thought. Ending with the key thought is stronger. Particularly in academic writing, we want our ideas to be strong.

Regardless, the one-two-three technique that we're using to *find* the end clause—and all the clauses, beginning and middle included—is, in the end, quite foolproof.

Beginning clausettes, middle clausettes, and end clausettes .Place commas between any and all clausettes and the main sentence. And make sure that your main sentence is a complete sentence, with a subject/noun (person, place, or thing) and predicate/verb (action).

So. Remember this. Because clause finding (and comma placing) is truly simple, once you identify your main sentence and comma-off the clausette.

Chapter 17

Add Two Complete Sentences to Create One Complete Sentence
a.k.a. One + One = One

Did you know that One + One = One? It's true—when talking about compound sentences.

A compound sentence is one complete sentence made of two complete sentences added together. Let me say that again. One sentence, made by two COMPLETE sentences added together.

Do you remember our conjunctions—our addition words? Conjunctions such as *and, but, for, so,* and *yet* are magic words that turn sentence mathematics around, to create One + One = One.

This chapter is short and sweet—because compound sentence math is short and sweet. Take one complete sentence (a sentence with a subject and predicate); take another complete sentence (a sentence with a subject and predicate) *that moves the first sentence's thought forward.* Now add the two together by placing a conjunction between.

Wait! Now comes the good part: Add your comma *before* the conjunction. Stand up and take a bow. One + One = One. You did it.

Now let's do some more sentence math together.

Example 1: *and*
"The legislator's assistant researched the bill, and the legislator chose to send the information to the committee on Thursday."
We have two sentences here:
1. The legislator's assistant researched the bill, and
2. the legislator chose to send the information to the committee on Thursday.

The *and* falls between the two complete sentences, and the comma comes before the "and." Super simple.

Example 2: *but*
"The director of the film received the nomination early, but the awards

committee presented the winners' announcement late."
We have two complete sentences here:
1. The director of the film received the nomination early, and
2. the awards committee presented the winners' announcement late.

The *but* falls between the two complete sentences, and the comma comes before the *but*.
It's the same idea as before, isn't it? And it's pretty easy to follow, right?

Example 3: *for*
"**According to the South Park Counseling Center, superstitions tend to inhibit the patients' ability to heal, for such recurring internal constraints root themselves into belief systems that patients find hard to dismiss.**"
We have two complete sentences here:
1. According to the South Park Counseling Center, superstitions tend to inhibit the patients' ability to heal, and
2. such recurring internal constraints root themselves into belief systems that patients find hard to dismiss.

The *for* falls between the two complete sentences, and the comma comes before the *for*. Yet one more time, the formula works.

Example 4: *so*
"**The Maori people inhabited neighboring New Zealand, so the native population from Australia who attended the conference identified with the examples, as well.**"
We have two complete sentences here:
1. The Maori people inhabited neighboring New Zealand, and
2. the native population from Australia who attended the conference identified with the examples, as well.

The *so* falls between the two complete sentences, and the comma comes before the *so*. The same formula works.

Example 5: *yet*
"**Nuclear power has been a part of the American landscape for years, yet many individuals continue to fear potential accidents with catastrophic results.**"
We have two complete sentences here:
1. Nuclear power has been a part of the American landscape for years, and
2. many individuals continue to fear potential accidents with catastrophic results.

The *yet* falls between the two complete sentences, and the comma comes before the *yet*. At this point, I'm sure you have the pattern down.

That was easy. Write two complete sentences attached by a conjunction that *move the reader forward into a new thought*, and you create One + One = One.

Chapter 18

Use "The One Less Rule" for Commas in Lists
a.k.a. Three in a Row Means Two to Go

When writing a list of three or more items, we must use commas to separate the items. The question is this: How many commas do we use?

To answer that question, we turn to *style guides*.

What's a style guide? I cover style guides really well in the *Simplified Research Writing* book, but for right now, all you have to know right now is that a style guide is basically a guide book of how-to-write rules, put together by an important group—the Big Cheeses of rule-book-making for writing. These books tell us all kinds of crazy details you never imagined you'd need to know. And, yes, the guides tell us where to put commas in a list of three or more items.

Problem is, some of the guides disagree with each other. With a list of three or more items, Strunk and White (authors of the classic, *The Elements of Style*) as well as Kate Turabian's guide (a.k.a. Chicago Style on steroids) both require commas to be placed between each of the items in the list. The American Psychological Association (APA) guide, the Modern Language Association Guide (MLA) and the American Medical Association (AMA) guide also say to place a comma between each item on the list. A few others leave the last comma out (I chat about it, below).

Who is right? Before we answer that question, let me introduce you to this famous last comma that everyone fights about....

And now, ladies and gentlemen, it's time to raise the curtain. Please welcome with me – the Oxford comma! (* Applause, applause * roar of the crowd *)

The Oxford comma is also called the *serial comma* or *Harvard comma*. According to Oxford Publishers, the Oxford comma is an "optional comma" [8] that is placed before the word *and*, at the end of a list. Traditionally used by

---

[8] http://www.oxforddictionaries.com/us/words/what-is-the-oxford-comma Accessed May 27, 2016.

printers, readers, and editors at Oxford University Press and Harvard University Press, those who use the Oxford comma do so for the clarity that it provides. You see, when you use the Oxford comma before the last item in a series, it separates or removes uncertainty or vagueness regarding the writer's intent. Because the last comma in a series can make or break the sentence's meaning.

Check out what happens in this sentence that does *not* use the Oxford comma: "I love my dogs, Carl and mom." So Carl and your mom are dogs? Oy! We need the Oxford comma, don't we? "I love my dogs, Carl, and mom" makes much more sense (even though it's still a bit strange to list the dogs along with mom....I'll try not to get too offended).

But the Oxford comma is a controversial figure. (Yes, there are some hecklers in the audience.) The Associated Press (AP) Stylebook used by American newspapers heads the pack, along with British and Australian guides. My advice is like most other college professors: Unless you write for a newspaper or live in Britain or Australia, use the Oxford comma. After all, I want clarity...don't you?

Here's a simple hands-on trick to remember to use the Oxford comma in a series: Raise your left hand. Stick your first three fingers into the air— yes, just three. Now raise your right hand. Put up only two fingers (like you're making a *peace* or *victory* sign). Now place the two fingers of your right hand in between the three fingers of your left hand; mesh the fingers, your right inside your left. Do you see how the fingers fit together?

Okay, now pay attention, because here's the point: Your left hand fingers are the three items in your "list of three," a series of items you've listed out in your sentence. Your two right hand fingers are your commas. Look at your fingers. In your list of three, your right hand fingers are exactly where your commas need to be: between your fingers.

Count the fingers on your right hand: One...two. Two fingers...two commas. Excuse the preschool teaching style. It's a memory device. Go with it.

Bottom line: We're talking about what I call *The One Less Rule* for commas in a list.

What if there are there four items in your list? Then the number of commas will be three (one less than four).

What about five items in a list? With five or more items, you'll probably want to use semicolons between items, instead of commas. (We'll go over this in the chapter on semicolons.)

Why semicolons? Because now our sentence is getting a little bit too long—and perhaps harder to follow, for your reader. Remember: Your job is to make reading *easy* for your reader, right? Semicolons make long lists easy on the eyes—and easy to understand.

I know that some of you are up in arms, panting heavily with frustration, because you were taught that you can leave the last comma out in your list of three. In fact, I'm absolutely positive that grammarphobes and die-hard English teachers are writhing in their seats, with cries of, "Wait a minute! Either way is proper!"

Technically, you're right. But here's the reason why I'm a stickler on the one-less rule: Clarity, clarity, clarity. Clarity is our war cry. Our job as a writer is to leave no question in the reader's mind.

The one-less rule leaves no questions.

The show is over... but wait, folks—the Oxford comma is coming back on stage for its curtain call. Yes, ladies and gentlemen, for one last time tonight, the Oxford commas is using The One Less Rule for commas in lists: item one...now we're putting in a comma...item two...there goes the second comma...item three...and there you go! A list of three in a row means two commas to go. Take a bow.

(Cheesy, I know. But I bet you remember it.)

SECTION 5

Punctuation:
It's all in the Details

Chapter 19

Keep End Punctuation Controlled and Snug
a.k.a. Experts Exclaim and Writers Know "Write Space"

It would be good for us to chat about two details that have to do with end punctuation. One item is the exclamation point; the other is end-of-sentence spacing. Don't worry, they're both short chats. Pull up a chair.

First, in academic writing, exclamation points are not allowed. That's right: They're not allowed. You can't use 'em. Never-ever. Oh, I know that you get excited and want to share that excitement with your professor. And I know that you want to make your point strong and memorable. But alas, it's true: You may not, not, *not* use exclamation points within your academic paper. Leave them out.

On the other hand, your quoted experts are *totally allowed* to use exclamation points. That's' right. Use a quote with an exclamation point inside of it, and everyone can have a party over it.

I agree: It's not fair. But those are the rules of the game.

Drop the exclamation points in your stuff, and keep the exclamation points inside of others' quoty-stuff. (Quoty. I made that one up, too. I kind of like it.)

In fact, a well-placed exclamation mark within your expert's quote doubles your instructors' point pizzazz—precisely because *you* didn't put in the exclamation point…the excited expert did. So, in the end, when the expert uses that dot with a tall skinny hat, it's really a great deal for you, the author.

Now let's go on to item number two. Item number two has to do with spacing. Here's the question: After end punctuation, how many spaces do we put on the page?

Ah, once again, we enter into the debate room. (It's the room next to the Oxford comma room.) The debate is between typewriting teachers of old and style guide users of new. Good news for us: The debate may be short-lived.

As of this book's publication, five style guides state that there is to be one, and only one, space after a period (full stop), question mark, and colon: *The Chicago Manual of Style; The Associated Press (AP) Stylebook; The American Psychological Association (APA) Publication Manual;* the *Gregg Reference Manual;* and the *Microsoft Manual of Style for Technical Publications* (the *MLA Handbook* can't decide and states both options.) That's a pretty hefty list of people telling us to put ONE SPACE after end punctuation.

So what's the hubbub about? I believe that old habits die hard. Us "old people" who learned to type on typewriters learned that we must type two spaces after end punctuation and colons. When did the end punctuation spacing change?

In typewriters of old, every typed letter was uniform in size. Typing two spaces after end punctuation helped to create clearer spacing for our eyes. Computers, on the other hand, give us proportional type: single letters aren't created as the same size. With the change in letter size, the result is an aesthetically-pleasing distance between punctuation marks and the surrounding letters. Using two spaces on a typewriter looked clearer, cleaner, and prettier. Make sense?

So what happens when we type two spaces on computers? Computers naturally make our letters squish together. When we put two spaces on a computer screen, the result is an illusion of a river of spaces flowing down our page...not what we want. Finally, there's another reason why the general populous has moved into the one-space rule: web site text.

Web site text writers and web designers need to fit more on the screen/page. Why? Because more words on the page means that the web site holds more of a chance to reel you in to a *click through* (buy) or a *come back* (return visit).

We all know that the Internet explosion created an information explosion. There are a bazillion web sites out there—each one trying to grab our attention. Web sites are built intentionally. Words on the page work with graphics to capture our eyes and hold us mesmerized within the page long enough to read the words. Then, if the web developer can get us reading (through effective text), the reader buys into the site's value.

Do you catch where I'm going with this? Page space on the Web is valuable. Two spaces after end punctuation wastes space, in their mind. Fewer end-punctuation spaces mean that more text fits on the page, meaning more letter space, more words—and more of a chance to grab a reader.

Now that we know the why of it all, it's time to get down to what to do about end punctuation. The answer's simple. After end punctuation, type only one space.

Yes, I know that old two-space habits die hard (we said that already). If you're having trouble kicking the habit, then make sure that when you're finished typing your document, use the Microsoft handy-dandy self-check.

It's easy to find and change out two-space endings for one-space endings. Go to the "Find and Replace" tool. Go to "Edit" on the navigational bar; now click on "Replace." A nifty "Find and Replace" box pops onto your screen. Within the "Find what" blank box, key in a period, followed by two spaces. Then, under the "Replace with" blank box, key in a period followed by one space. Hit "Replace All" and watch the magic. Every single one of your two-space typos in your document turn to one-space wonders.

Of course, there may be an exception to our one-space rule. Courier fonts (and some others) are mono-spaced fonts, like the typewriters of old. When using a mono-spaced font, consult your instructor for his or her preference for spacing with end punctuation.

Thanks for the chat. Now you know: After periods, question marks, and colons....stick with the right writing space. One.

EB Conroy, MA, MFA

Chapter 20

Keep it Inside the Quotes
a.k.a. Plant End Punctuation on the Correct Side of the Fence

Quotation marks present tricky situations for punctuation. The goal of this chapter is for you to look at end punctuation with a simplistic, easy-peasy perspective. I want you to feel comfortable with where to put those quotation marks—while keeping end punctuation within the rules.

First, let's talk about when *not* to use quotation marks. In academic pieces, when you put in information that is not someone's exact words, you cannot use quotation marks around that information. (* I'm making "air quotes" right now. You know them, right? Okay. That's what we're talking about.)

I don't mean to talk down to you on things you probably know already, but too many people will summarize and re-word other people's direct words, and they still feel compelled to throw up those silly-ol' quotation marks. Not necessary.

Use quotation marks only when you're writing down someone's exact words.

Second, let's talk about interrupting your quotation. *Interrupting* the quotation means putting something that's *not* quoted *between* quoted words.

In writing a quote, interrupting is not considered rude; it's considered a technique. Some of us like to place part of the quote down on paper, then step aside with a *she said* or *he stated.* Next, we pick up the quote where we left off.

Here's what's important to note: If we're continuing on with a quote, we do not capitalize the second part of the quotation.

Let me show you what it looks like.

Wrong example: "Rich uncles are far and few between," stated Mr.

Cunningham, "**And**, in our family's case, we actually have one."
Right example: "Rich uncles are far and few between," stated Mr. Cunningham, "**and**, in our family's case, we actually have one."

Easy to understand. Hard to remember to do.

Third, let's approach the tricky *quote within a quote* situation. If you're crazy enough to have found a quote within a quote, then you'll need to use single quotation marks for the quotation within the quotation. I say "crazy enough" because academic writers are supposed to seek what's called *primary information*—info that's straight from the speaker's mouth, not secondhand words. Primary information is strong; secondary information is weak. Go for the strong.

But sometimes we have to be crazy. Sometime's all we have is a secondary quote. No worries. If you *have* to have a quote within a quote, then do it this way:

Right example:
Senator Haverson explained, "When I spoke with the mayor of the city, the mayor said, 'The crisis is the worst that we've experienced in the past 20 years.'"

Did you see how that worked? The part that someone else said had *single quotation marks* around it. ('The crisis is the worst that we've experienced in the past 20 years.') The *entire thing*, which is all of Senator Haverson's quote, has *double quotation marks* around it—because he actually said the whole enchilada. And the whole enchilada is his exact words. (The " mark comes before the entire shebang, and the the " mark comes after the entire shebang.)

Now here's the most important point of this chapter: Periods and commas *go inside your quotation marks*. Yup.

(Well…almost always. The only time that your period or comma *won't* be inside the quotation marks is if you have to show people where you got information—you have to show your source—and you have a parenthetical reference following your quote. You're in overload now, you say? Hey, seriously, don't worry about this entire paragraph. You'll learn about parenthetical references in the *Simplified Research Writing* book. And this exception with end punctuation is only with research writing, in specific situations. So I don't even know why I just freaked you out with that unnecessary information. * facepalm)

Here are three examples of the right way to use periods within quotation marks:

Right example 1: Carson stated, "Absolutely. We know how to run the corporation and will continue to do so."

Right example 2: Throughout history, falconry continues to be a sport practiced by both royalty and "country commoners."

Right example 3: Anderson, supporting counseling practices within the church, writes, "The more that trained men and women positively infiltrate the church with their godly influence, the more hope that we have that the wounded will heal" (69). Ooops. That's the parenthetical reference thingy. The (69) is the page where the reader will find the quote, in the referenced source. And the period goes after the reference. Well, at least you see what it looks like. Now erase it from your mind....

Here's a factoid for you: If you live in England, you'll want to place commas and periods *outside* the quotation marks. Why the difference? The reason resounds around purely stylistic preferences. *Outside the quotation marks* is the English way.

Think of it like this: Americans play football. In order to score in football, you need to put the football into the End Zone. Now imagine: The place where the bleachers *meet* the End Zone is where the quotation marks go. For our word picture, consider the football as the period. To score, we place the period into the End Zone—not into the stands. Place the football (period) into the End Zone (seats), and you score. Don't place the football (period) *beyond* the End Zone. Stay *in* the End Zone.

Silly word picture.

Yes, the redundancy is thick. It's because the *period in the End Zone* thing is one of the most common errors that I experience while correcting college papers—and I don't want you do be among the crowd.

Bottom line: When it comes to end punctuation, remember where in the world you're standing (or writing to). Because your location influences where you put end punctuation. This is an American book, so we put the period inside the quotation marks.

Now. One more thing.

Colons and semicolons mess up the rules a bit. Colons and semicolons go outside closing quotation marks. Don't panic. Here's what I mean:

Right example 1: "Baker condemned the event as 'weak political gerrymandering'; Culver and her colleagues agreed through a quote in the *Washington Times* but did not engage in the debate."

Right example 2: Connor included three reasons for his successful "medical track record": training, education, and hospital efficiency.

You see? The semicolon and colon aren't inside the quotation marks; they're outside.

What about question marks? Question marks stay with action. If what's inside the quotation marks is a question, then put the question mark inside. If what's outside the quotation marks is a question, then put the question mark outside. Here's what I mean:

Wrong example 1: The reporter asked, "What is your stance on the subject"? Oops. Wrong. (* Insert buzzer sound here)

The question is inside of the quotation marks, so the question mark belongs like this:

Right example 1: The reporter asked, "What is your stance on the subject?"

Here's another one...

Wrong example 2: Will the campaign cover "economic hardship?"
Oops again. The question is, "Will the campaign cover?" The question mark goes with the question.

So the words, "economic hardship," stay away from the question mark, like this:

Right example 2: Will the campaign cover "economic hardship"?
Now that's better. Follow what appears to be logical. Put the question mark where the question resides.

Be in the know: If you live in the US, plant your end punctuation on the right side of the fence...and that's the IN side.

Chapter 21

Advance your Punctuation: The Comma, Ellipses, and Em Dash Relationship
a.k.a. Pause, Wait, and Throw it Forward

Did you know that punctuation has a dial for speed? That's right. In writer's terms, punctuation means motion—or lack thereof. We all learned in kindergarten that a period means *stop*. But I'm here to tell you that when it comes to driving the pace of your paper, there's so much more to punctuation than you may have first imagined.

Commas

The *comma*, which we tackled in our last chapters, is a pause. I don't mean that the comma is like the pause button on your DVD player—because many of us pause with the remote, then go into the kitchen to get a snack, only to end up there for five minutes or more while putting together a mini meal. That kind pause is way too long. The comma pause that I'm talking about is simply a breath pause. Breathe, and then go again. That's what I mean by a comma pause.

Don't get me wrong: I'm not saying to put a comma where you feel there should be a pause. We already talked about the right way to figure out where to put in your commas. But some actually teach writers to plop in commas "wherever you need to take a breath, or wherever you feel a pause." Gah, no. Don't do it. That's terrible advice—and it's backwards. Commas, placed in their proper places in your paper, create pauses. Pauses don't create commas.

Make sense? Good.

Ellipses

***Ellipses* are the three or four dots meaning that something is left out, or there's a literal wait in conversation…like this.** The ellipses that I used in the last sentence mean that time passed, and time-passing dots are used in fiction writing and commentary-type writing (like I'm writing now). The time-passing ellipses create a wait longer than the pausing comma. However, within academic writing, we use ellipses only within in-text or block quotations, to tell the reader that we skipped over and left out some text (because it wasn't needed). Otherwise, we don't use ellipses in academic writing. They're out of the game's action. Ellipses can join the exclamation mark on the bench.

Here's an example of leaving out text within a quotation: "The commander of the unit spoke hastily, creating confusion in the ranks and…according to the trial transcripts, the commander's actions created a lack of credibility." (That's a made-up example.)

The three dots in my quotation mean that I left out some words from the sentence. The original sentence was longer, but I didn't need to put everything in the original sentence into my paper. So when the reader reads my quote, I (as the writer) am not going to confuse the reader with extra fluff that doesn't support the point of my paragraph. (We don't want to distract our reader with insignificant info, do we?) With ellipses, the reader continues to follow the writer's line of thought, and we're focused together: The writer only shares what's important, and the reader only gets what's important. Everybody wins.

But we still have to show that something was left out, just to be polite. Ellipses are polite little guys, tipping their hat to the information left on the bench, as the parts not entering our game.

I can also use *four* dots, to represent the end of a sentence (the fourth and last dot is a period). Here's an example: "The commander of the unit spoke hastily, creating confusion in the ranks and distrust among the troops…. According to the trial manuscripts, the commander's actions created a lack of credibility." In the previous sentences, the four dots mean that words were taken out *and* a sentence ended. The word *according* starts the next sentence.

Choosing three dots or four dots makes a difference. But whether you use the three or four dot version, the *speed* of time passing is the same: the dots give us a brief waiting period that notes the absence of words. It's like a deep breath. (The pace can be a tad bit slower than a comma.) There we go again, showing how punctuation can match up with speed or pace.

Hyphens

Now let's talk about the *hyphen*. Hyphenated words use the little dash that's found on your keyboard, stuck on the bottom part of the key that's to the right of the zero key. Placed between words, the single dash mark is called a hyphen. Words like *two-thirty* and *real-life* use a hyphen. Hyphens don't change the reader's pace, really. Hyphens smush two words together as one.

Hyphens actually look small, as stick-together bits between two words. The single, short pieces touch the words on either side. Do you see it, in *stick-together*?

I'll be straight with you: Hyphens have a whole-lotta rules. I'm not going to cover all the rules all here. When you're wondering if you need a hyphen, you'll have to do what I and everyone else on the planet often does: Look 'em up. Frankly, I don't want to memorize all the hyphen rules. I want to save my brain space for more amazing things.

But, hey, we need to know a few hyphen types. So here are a couple of common hyphen rules that we use every day.

One common hyphen is the stuck-together adjectives hyphen. Remember, adjectives describe nouns. The two stuck-together adjectives are called *compound adjectives*—and *compound* means *two or more parts added together*, right? It makes sense.

Here are examples of compound adjectives stuck together, to describe a noun: "Monster" is a noun (a thing). If I want to describe the monster's height, I might say it's a "twelve-foot, multi-scaled monster." If I want to describe the fact that my pet monster can roam my property and devour as many bugs as it likes, I might call my monster a "free-range monster." Two adjectives, stuck together, to describe my noun. Easy.

We can stick two nouns together. You see it all the time. Commander-in-Chief. Son-in-law. Passer-by. Three-year-old.

We can also stick two verbs together, to "make a funny," as my brother says. Verbs are action words, right? I can make one action word, out of two words. I might say, my monster "flip-flopped" over the rocks and "jibber-jabbered" with the birds in the trees.

Some hyphens come attached to bits of words of "ex" and "mid." *Ex-girlfriend, ex-roommate, mid-week,* and *mid-state* are all examples of attachment hyphens.

Number words from twenty-one to ninety-nine use hyphens. We see it (and use them) every day.

EB Conroy, MA, MFA

And I love the special uses of hyphens. Like when you have three of the same letter together, and a hyphen simply makes the word easier to read. *I enjoyed the fall-like weather* is a good example sentence, where the hyphen helps our eyes not turn into black-and-white spirals. And single-letter attachments like x-rays, A-frame houses, and e-zine magazines in your email box all use hyphens.

Some day, I'll make a fun little hyphen how-to guide. But for now, if you're ever confused about whether or not to use a hyphen, look it up.

En Dashes and Em Dashes

An en dash is a bit longer line than a hyphen. It's used as a tool to throw the reader forward. The en dash looks like this – with space between the word and the little-bit-longer dash.

An *em dash*, on the other hand, is an elongated line that touches the words—like this. The em dash's job is the same as an en dash. It just looks longer.

The difference between a *hyphen* and the *en* and *em dash* is not only the length but also the use. The *en* and *em dashes* throw the reader forward—like this.

I admit it: I use a lot of em dashes. They're a bit addicting. Em dashes are becoming more popular in magazine-type writing and even academic writing. I believe that the purpose of the *en* and *em dash* is to create more speed, tossing the reader forward into the next word or phrase.

That's my opinion. A professor from my MFA program believed that the en and em dash, when used in place of parentheses, feels as slow as parentheses. You be the judge. Either way, the en dash or em dash separates text, causing a change in speed.

So which dash—the en dash or the em dash—is the right one to use? Books texts use the em dash. Magazines' use varies, per a particular magazine's editors' guidelines (and preferences). In college, if you want to "do it right," the best bet for you is to check the style guide for your particular academic institution. And, as always, ask your instructor if he or she has a preference. Then follow it. Warning: Some professors don't know the difference between an en dash and an em dash. So don't be surprised if you ask, and the instructor looks at you sideways. In that case, do what you like and par-tay.

A word of caution: Em dashes can be overused, overworked, and overrated. Check out professional writers' use of the em dash. Try not to get carried away and start throwing the little lines onto your paper like a mascot at a football game throwing out free t-shirts.

OH—and one last thing: When using Microsoft Word, your computer automatically creates en dashes for you. It's magic.

Here's how you do it.
Simply type a word;
then type a space;
then type the hyphen (the single little dash to the right of the zero key);
then type another space;
then type your next word.

As soon as you finish typing the last word and hit the space key, your en dash turns into an en dash, like this: –.

If you want an em dash to magically appear, then don't type the spaces.
Type a word;
then immediately type two dashes;
then immediately type the next word;
then type a space.

Bam. As soon as you type the last space, the em dash appears. Magic.

If at any point in the process you hit a different key or go back a space, then the magic won't work. You'll end up with a single dash, like this: -. So make sure that you follow the formula for the magic em dash to appear.

Warning: In many email systems and in typescript, the magical en or em dash transformation won't happen. So we type two dashes side by side -- with the result looking like the two dashes in this sentence that I just typed, with no spaces between the dashes but, yes, spaces on either side of the dashes. Published books' em dashes look like this—magically created.

Wow—it's amazing, isn't it? You get to choose the speed of your text by adjusting the punctuation, as in a pause...ellipses—and en or em dashes. There are a few more speed-creating punctuation marks coming up. In the meantime, before we get to those chapters, play with the dashes a bit. But be careful; you might find yourself having fun with it.

EB Conroy, MA, MFA

Chapter 22

Use Stuck-Together Semicolon Sentences
a.k.a. Closely-Connected Cousins Shake Hands

For some reason, semicolons (next to dashes) have become my best friends. I like them…probably *too* much. There's something friendly about semicolons. I like friendly.

Seriously, semicolons are all about connection. When two sentences stand closely related, the semicolon becomes the handshake between the two sentences. But it's not just any handshake, mind you; there is a relationship between the two sentences. I like to call the two sentences cousins.

Here's the story: The two cousins haven't seen each other in a while. The first cousin walks in with a big smile, grasps the hand of the second cousin, pumps his cousin's hand (and arm) up and down, and bellows, "How 'ya doin', cuz? So great to see ya!" We know that the second cousin is going to respond to the first…and we can't wait to hear what the second cousin has to say. After all, the two know each other well—and they haven't seen each other in a while. Wouldn't *you* be excited to share the latest and greatest?

The semicolon gives that kind of *anticipation*: The reader knows that the idea within the first sentence isn't complete (just like the conversation between the two cousins isn't complete). And so—finally—the second cousin speaks. Ahhhh—now we feel complete. We experienced the second part of the conversation; the two cousins experienced a full-circle moment.

The cousins and the sentences have a lot in common. Cousins are two separate people; the sentences on either side of the semicolon are two separate (and complete) sentences. Cousins can stand alone, independent, without the other in sight; the two sentences can stand alone, independent, without the other in sight. The cousins are equally significant persons, in their own right; the sentences are equally significant statements of thought, in their own right.

I really don't have to give you examples of semicolon handshakes with the cousins. Take a look around this chapter; I've planted examples everywhere.

Don't use semicolons with cousin sentences connected by the words "and," "or," and "but." The job of connecting sentences, using conjunctions between the two, goes to the comma.

Wrong example: According to *USA Today*, the pickle processing plant won the award; and the owner of the company was pleasantly surprised.
Right example: According to *USA Today*, the pickle processing plant won the award, and the owner of the company was pleasantly surprised.
Right example, using a semicolon: According to *USA Today*, the pickle processing plant won the award; the owner of the company was pleasantly surprised.

Here's another semicolon specialty to note: The semicolon handshake connecting two cousin sentences can be followed by a *conjunctive adverb*.

Oh my, **I hear you saying.** *Here we go.* *We're jumping into those unbearable English grammar words.* Chill. Don't close the book. It's only two words. And they're easy to understand. (Breathe.)

A conjunctive adverb is a word that commonly falls after a semicolon, as a nifty connector. *Con* means *with*. *Junct* means *meeting together* (as in *junction*). And *ive* means *action*. So the nifty word is all about making sentences meet together, with action. Conjunctive adverbs. Simple.

Again—No worries, friendly-but-sensitive grammarphobes; there's no need to be terrified or even intimidated. Believe it or not, you already know the words falling into the conjunctive adverb category. I've broken down the list of conjunctive adverbs below, based on the higher language that we want to use in academic writing.

The following are my opinions, mind you; however, the lists might prove helpful in choosing the right word at the right time, no matter what category the words are placed within.

Higher word **conjunctive adverbs**
however
therefore
consequently
otherwise
likewise
similarly
finally

Can be considered strange for today
moreover
nonetheless
nevertheless

Conjunctive adverbs of a level a little lower than academic
also
again
namely

Conversational (and not recommended)
still
besides
then
that is
incidentally

Each of the conjunctive adverbs above are uber-cool connectors for our academic papers. Each can be used in the second half of a semicolon-using sentence. Place the conjunctive adverb after the semicolon, at the beginning of the second full sentence. And always, always, always use a comma after the conjunctive adverb.

Here are more examples:
* The presidential candidate was slated to arrive at noon**; however,** Air Force One didn't land until two-thirty in the afternoon.
* The plane was late**; therefore,** we had to push back the time of the first speaking engagement.
* The plane was late**; consequently,** we had to push back the time of the first speaking engagement.
* Four Secret Service agents kept watch on the main roads**; similarly,** Air Force helicopters kept a perimeter in the air space above the airport.
* Four Secret Service agents kept watch on the main roads**; likewise,** Air Force helicopters kept a perimeter in the air space above the airport.

Pretty nifty, eh?

Finally, there are a four additional conjunctive adverbs that I recommend academic writers shy from:
* *Indeed* and *furthermore*: Both words are a bit stuffy and can send an I'm-above-you feeling from the writer to the reader.
* *Thus* and *hence*. Both feel King-James-Bible-ish—or like Ben Franklin's going to jump off the page and wink at you. Let's stay in our century, shall

EB Conroy, MA, MFA

we?

So what do conjunctive adverbs do for pace and speed for the reader, anyway? The conjunctive adverb throws the reader forward. The relationship feels stronger, with more comparison or contrast...or cause and effect. Most importantly, conjunctive adverbs (placed after semicolons), help your text gather speed.

Semicolons have one more job to do; they connect items in a gargantuan list. Okay, not gargantuan...but long. With long lists, comma after comma can look mighty confusing (and the commas get tired); so the semicolons take over...like a relay race.

Here's what a sentence looks like when you use *comma after comma* (the wrong example): *Four candidates stood together on stage: Robert J. Jones, president of Exfixion, Corinne P. Lambert, Vice President of Clanderson Corporation, Paulette Brackman, President of the Schmillern Company, and Joseph K. Mandel, Chief Executive Officer of Rugman and Rugman.*

Eek. That's confusing.

Here's the same sentence, using *semicolons* (the right example): *Four candidates stood together on stage: Robert J. Jones, president of Exfixion; Corinne P. Lambert, Vice President of Clanderson Corporation; Paulette Brackman, President of the Schmillern Company; and Joseph K. Mandel, Chief Executive Officer of Rugman and Rugman.*

Ahh. That's much better. The sentence still has a crazy amount of info, but at least (with the semicolons) we can decipher and find the meaning.

Here's another sentence using the *wrong-way* comma after comma construction: *The president of the corporation visited construction sites in Chicago, Illinois, Atlanta, Georgia, Houston, Texas, and Los Angeles, California.*

Ooh, that's messy. And hard to understand.

Here's the same sentence, using *right-way* semicolons: *The president of the corporation visited construction sites in Chicago, Illinois; Atlanta, Georgia; Houston, Texas; and Los Angeles, California.*

Right. Now I get it.

Finally, glance over this last comma after comma *poor* example: *Visitors* *to the home admired its unique features, including the eight-foot oak table in the dining room, the rough-hewn beams and arches in the great hall, the polished brass knobs created by a local craftsman, the hand-braided rugs laid throughout the bedrooms, and the floor-length draperies throughout the first and second floors.*

Hmm. A lotta great info resides in that there house (said with a twang). But you and I both know—it's too *long*. How can I fix the sentence, to make it clear (and correct)? And can it be accomplished without taking away the length?

Sure can, with the magic of semicolons.

I bring you the closing right-way semicolon example: *Visitors to the home admired its unique features, including the eight-foot oak table in the dining room; the rough-hewn beams and arches in the great hall; the polished brass knobs created by a local craftsman; the hand-braided rugs laid throughout the bedrooms; and the floor-length draperies throughout the first and second floors.*

Phew *wipes brow. Much better.

To close, I present a challenge: Within this chapter, how many semicolons can you find?

Chapter 23

Use the Here-it-is Colon
a.k.a. Point Me to the Answer

I admit, throughout this book, I've used colons liberally. Though the colon is not as special to me as the semicolon, I like the guy quite a bit—because he does things that no other punctuation mark can do. He's direct. He can bring things to a stop. And then he tells it like it is.

The colon is an announcer. He's the host or hostess introducing the song or the next guest. He sets you up for what's to come. I love it. I know that something's coming, and that helps me to make a mental note to expect key information: the stuff that matters. How easy for me—and you.

It's true: The colon is a punctuation mark that anyone—including you—can learn to love.

We learn to love the colon because he's so *helpful*. The colon doesn't *only* announce; he also waves a flag and tells us to pay attention to what's coming. He says, "Okay, now—sit up and take notice. Here comes the *best* part yet...." And we all fall for it. There's no way that we'll *not* fall for it; he grabs our attention every time. It's all about emphasis. The colon's entire existence is to help us get ready for the punch line.

And the colon is versatile. He can announce one word...two words...a phrase...a sentence...a list...a paragraph...a section...even graphically-laid-out information in an article...oy! You *gotta* love it!

To my horror, I read a web site today where the author claimed that colons are nearly obsolete. What?! Colons aren't necessary?! Yikes! The writer of that article can't possibly know the colon that I know.

When do I use a colon? I use a colon when I want to point to something. The colon sticks out its finger and says, "There! There it is!" The colon is on the lookout to show you, the reader, the exact answers and solutions you're seeking. However, I must warn you: To make the colon truly work, the portion after the colon must meet simple guidelines. What are the guidelines? The pointed-to info must explain (spell out what came before) or itemize details.

Here's what I mean:
(How cool, I just used a colon…)

Example 1 (pointing to one word)
Only one of the subjects at the elementary school was taught twice a day: mathematics.
The colon pointed his finger right to the answer: math.

Example 2 (pointing to two words)
The store carried only one brand: Tommy Hilfiger.

Again, the colon pointed his finger right to the answer: the clothing brand, Tommy Hilfiger.

Example 3 (pointing to a phrase)
The senator kept one item in his pocket at all times: a bottle of hand sanitizer.

The colon points toward what the senator keeps tucked away: the answer to the senator's obsessive compulsive need to keep his hands away from all-pervasive germs. How simple can we get?

Example 4 (pointing to a list)
Chief Executive Officer Brandel stated that there are three factors keeping the Smarto Company from excelling within the marketplace: the distributors' inability to break into established markets, the sales personnel's lack of understanding of the benefits of the products, and the buyers' hesitation to switch brands.

Ooh-la-la, what a set up! The colon points toward the three factors: a list of three long phrases separated by commas. Brilliant.

Example 5 (pointing to a quotation)
Madison begins his speech with a call to action: "Citizens, take heart! Now is the time to listen and take action!"

What a nice technique, eh?

Example 6 (pointing to a block quotation, also called an offset quote)
According to Smith, the answer is obvious:

> *After double spacing and indenting, the quotation goes here…without quotation marks and without italics, if we want to get technical…but I'm getting ahead of myself. You'll have to buy* Simplified Research Writing *to get the whole*

enchilada on offset quotations... and if this were a real-life offset quote, it wouldn't be italicized...and I'd have to write five lines, so that's why I'm running on and on and on...to meet the five line minimum criteria that most style guides insist upon, for using an offset quote. Oh, wait...I already put in five lines. We can move on now.

Example 7 (pointing to an explanation)
The instructions within the manual are simple: Place the pin into the slot and then turn the mechanism clockwise.

Note that we can capitalize what comes *after* the colon—if what comes after is a complete sentence. I say *can* because capitalizing a complete sentence isn't really a rule at all; capitalizing is a *preference* or *matter of style*. However, the true rule is that if what comes after the colon is *not* a complete sentence, you *may not* capitalize. As always, check with your handy-dandy professor-preferred style guide for specifics.

When it comes to colons, sometimes we make the silliest mistakes.
First, we may think that colons work when verbs are in the picture. But colons don't belong after verbs.

Here are some wrong examples of colon use (because the verb gets in the way):

Wrong example 1
Regarding history resources, Paul Jonas' favorite libraries are: Purdue, Yale, and the University of Michigan.
The correction (because the verb *are* takes out the need for the colon)
Regarding history resources, Paul Jonas' favorite libraries are Purdue, Yale, and the University of Michigan.

Wrong example 2
The voters' information packet came with: two brochures, one "I voted" sticker, and one envelope.
The correction (because the sentence is a normal construction and needs no colon)
The voters' information packet came with two brochures, one "I voted" sticker, and one envelope.

The second mistake: Don't use sentence fragments before colons.
"What if: the answer is too easy," doesn't cut it (the use of the colon in that sentence is wrong...please don't copy what I wrote and say that you saw it in a book). We need a complete sentence before the colon.

Finally, here is a list of a few itsy-bitsy academic-paper places where colons like to hide:
In time... 3:30
In ratios... 2:1
In URLs... http://ww.nameofwebsitegoeshere.com
In the Bible... John 3:16
Between titles and subtitles... *Journey Home: A Father's Story of Love*
In references such as footnotes, endnotes, and bibliographies... New York: Vintage Books

In academic writing, some colons hide in places we rarely visit.
Dialogue in plays and screenplays, advanced mathematics, computer language, dictionary definitions, and so on, conceal colons. However, the book you're reading right now won't touch on the hideaways. If your college course needs you to delve into such caches, then put on your detective hat and jump onto the web.

Now that you're a bit more familiar with my friend, the Here-it-is Colon, I hope you'll hang with him on occasion. Take my word for it: He can add a lot of fun—and clarity—to your writing.

Chapter 24

Recognize the Finer Points
a.k.a. Don't Let the Little Guys Bring Your Grade Down

Sometimes it's the little things that count …against your grade, that is. I don't want to be a spoilsport, but now is probably a good time to talk about the finer points of academic writing. If we want our writing to shine, then we need to contend with simple mistakes that add up to big point losses.

I'll be frank with you: When your instructors grade your papers, there are three general ways that he or she approaches grading. First, your instructor looks for good *content*. Do you have content that makes sense? Is the content arranged well? Do your paper's points follow a sound line of thinking? Second, your instructor notes what's *not* there. What's missing? What did you leave out? What should be there, to support your argument, fill in the gaps, and bolster your point? Third, your instructor looks for what I call *the mess-ups*.

Yes, it's true. Your professor has his or her eye out for those little errors to tally mark—those little problems slipping in between the lines like weeds in sidewalk cracks. Grammar errors. Punctuation errors. And finer-point detail errors.

Don't get me wrong: We're not standing poised with our red pen, face scowling and an evil laugh rising from a curled lip. No, no—that's not it at all. We're simply and matter-of-factly poised with our red pen, peacefully alert, ready to *help* you by correcting issues that threaten your writing.

When I meet a class full of writing students for the first time, I let them know that I love to mark up their papers. Yes, the more marks, the merrier; the more corrections, the more that they can correct. The more feedback provided, the more growth that can occur. As I explain my scary-but-wonderful point to the students, the initial look of horror fades from shell-shocked to skeptical-but-wanting-to-believe-me.

I go on: How can you become a better writer if you don't have someone showing you what needs to change? Yes, it's hard to take correction. It's hard for me, too (making corrections take oodles of time). But it's necessary. The both of us might as well look at such fine-point correction as positive.

EB Conroy, MA, MFA

Finer points are some of the easiest corrections to make. And once you know what to do right, you can do the same again and again.

The finer points **are those simple little pieces of learning that we can memorize.** You say you struggle with memorization? Then the next best thing is to know where to go—to be able to look up the answers quickly. And with Google-esque finesse, finding answers is lickety-split easy. Though the content's grandiose points and fantastic framework of our paper are important, at some crucial point, we want to take out the magnifying glass and look at the intimate details.

Let's review a few.

Brackets. What are brackets for, anyway? Brackets, those square-ish little guys, show up in word-for-word quotes. As the author of the academic work, much of your job is to clarify another person's information, for your reader.

Brackets help us add clarifying information to a quote. When writing a quote that you believe isn't totally clear to the reader, you're allowed to add words, to clarify. But you have to let the reader know *which words are the original text* (verbatim) and *which text is the author-added part.*

How? The way we show the reader what was added is simple: We place brackets around the added info. It's a good thing.

Get this: Here's a real-life business scenario that might happen to real-life people like you and me in real life. Really. (It's life.) I'm talking about an event where you or I would need to correct someone else's writing, by adding information within brackets. Let's use a story. Stories are fun.

Here we go. Let's say Sally, a business trip coordinator for a highfalutin company, sends a memo to Kyle. Kyle is the scheduler, for getting the boss scheduled with a limousine that will take him to the airport, to catch a flight. You with me so far?

But there's a problem. The original memo from Sally to Kyle states, "Mr. Howard's limousine should pick him up at three o'clock, for the fight is scheduled to leave the airport just before six." Kyle's job, after getting the memo, is to forward the information on to the limo company via an email scheduling service. It's all written word communication.

But Kyle's confused. When's the flight leaving? Are we talking about AM or PM? It's not stated in the memo. So Kyle calls Sally and asks, *are you talkin'* *about early morning or late afternoon?* Sally says, *Oops. Sorry, I meant to put in AM.*

Before forwarding the email to the limo scheduling service, Kyle employs the bracket fix. He goes into the email and adds brackets, like so: "Mr. Howard's limousine should pick him up at three o'clock [AM], for the flight is scheduled to leave the airport just before six [AM]." If the original text didn't say AM or PM, the reader might assume Mr. Howard was picked up at three in the afternoon—because who wants to get up at three AM, right? The brackets make the crazy super-early flight time clear. Especially if Kyle is supposed to get Mr. Howard his early-morning coffee in the hotel lobby, before the limo arrives.

Sally and Kyle's example was somewhat informal. So Kyle might not have had to use brackets—perhaps he could have simply added the information before hitting *send*. But in super-formal business situations, the brackets might be required. You never know. And in your essays and papers, when quoting someone and you need to add clarifying information, you hafta-gotta-really-must use brackets.

Dates… AD precedes and BC follows. That's right. The two special upper-case letters fall in different places. If I'm writing about an event that happened AD, then I write AD 500; if I write a number that is BC, then I write 500 BC. And did you notice the lack of periods in the two letters? It's now acceptable to not use periods.

Let's all get on the same page about *AD*. AD does not stand for *after death* (as in, after the death of Jesus Christ…although the idea is useful, to remember which is which). The letters AD actually stand for *anno Domini*, Latin for *in the year of our Lord*. And, by the way, you won't find the BC/AD system of dating in the Bible; a theologian created the Gregorian calendar system in the 6th Century. The Gregorian calendar begins with the year AD 1 as the calculated year that Jesus Christ was believed to have been born. (Note: Some scholars now believe that Jesus was actually born between the years AD 2 and AD 6.) Yes, BC does stand for *before Christ*. Yes, it is a Christian dating system. Yes, the system has been used worldwide since about the 11th Century. Now that we have history straight, let's always write AD *before* the year's number and BC *after* the year's number.

More dates… BCE and CE both follow their numbers. BCE stands for *Before Common Era*; CE stands for *Common Era*. AD and CE are the same thing; BC and BCE are the same thing. Many believe that in the 1800s, people decided to get politically correct and not base dates on any one faith or religion—though some say the move to BCE-CE notations began as early as the 1600s. Regardless, the practice ramped up in the 1980s (fairly recently). Some believe that the CE-BCE notations are an affront to Christianity; others do not. That's something you'll have to decide. For writing in your essays and papers, simply check with your school or university, to know which to use.

Confused? Don't be. Here's the trick: Only AD is written before the number. All the rest of the letters (BC, BE, and BCE) are written after the number. Since letter A begins the alphabet, occupying the *first* letter's place, it's easy to think of AD as coming *first*. Make sense?

Time…AM and PM. Or a.m. and p.m. When do you use what? Is there a difference between the two? According to *The Everyday Writer*, a writing text by Andrea Lunsford, modern writers are doing away with the periods on a number of abbreviations. To that, I say, "Woo-hoo!" Less is best, in my book. I like keyboard economy. Write AM and PM.

Single quotes within double quotes. (Yes, we've already talked about this one. But it bears repeating in our details section.)

For normal quotes (that's pretty much anything that you're quoting from an expert source), use the regular-old quotation marks: double lines on either side. When something else is quoted inside your quote, use single quotation marks around the inside stuff. Check out this example:

> According to the company president's notes on the matter, "The irritated accountant stated that the original numbers were what they call 'super-duper-over-inflated' and, therefore, not to be trusted."

Keep the double quotes on the *extreme outside*; place single quotes on any quoted material *inside*. And, please please please don't use single quotes all by their little lonesome. They don't like to be alone. They *have* to go inside the double quotes, at all times. Thanks.

Footnote numbers. Where do footnote numbers go? You'll find more about footnotes in the *Simplified Research Writing* book. For now, know to place footnote numbers at the end of the sentence or portion quoted, *outside the punctuation* and *outside the quotation marks*. That means after periods. Right up against the word, without a space.

Like this:
Example 1: The containers were shipped every Monday and Friday.[9]

---

[9] This footnote would show where the fact, "The containers were shipped every

Example 2: According to Ms. Thomas' testimony on the witness stand, "Monday and Friday—those are the days. The company always came by first thing in the morning, and that's what happened the day he was shot."[10]

(Read the footnotes below, for commentary on the correct use of the footnote number.)

Slashes. In your text, don't use 'em: No him/her, either/or, yes/no, or any other slash combination. In your web addresses, use 'em: Your http:// has to have the slashes or the link won't work.

Capitalization. Here's the list:

1. *Proper nouns*: Gotta' have 'em: people, nationalities, ethnic groups, places, structures, ships, aircraft, organizations, institutions, historical events, eras, trade names—anything that is specific must be capitalized.

2. *Titles attached to specific names* must be capitalized: Doctor Jones, Chief Justice Peterman, and Professor E.B. Conroy (that's me).

3. *Titles of works:* books, stories, articles, speeches, poems, documents, paintings, musical pieces, paintings, plays, and musicals…all have to be capitalized.

4. *InterCaps:* Yes, sometimes the middle of a special name has a capital letter: iTunes, iPod, FedEx, eBay…all fall under the nifty name of *InterCaps*. And all have a special place in the writer's heart (or should I say the shift key's heart).

5. *Title caps:* Let's not forget title caps: In titles, the important are capitalized. Don't capitalize words itsy-bitsy words like *the* and *it*. And, by the way, the first and last word of a title are ALWAYS capitalized, no matter the size or importance.

6. *No-No caps:* Finally, don't ever use all caps like I did in the last sentence (ALWAYS). I did it to make a point. The use of all caps for emphasis (trying

---

Monday and Friday," came from. Notice how the number for the footnote is smack-dab next to the end punctuation (the period). There are no spaces between the period and the little number.

[10] Ah, now we have a murder case! Oy! Ms. Thomas' testimony would be footnoted. Check out how the little footnote number is smack-dab up against the last quotation mark. That's how you do it, with no extra spaces.

to be dramatic) does not exist in academia-land.

Abbreviations. If you want to abbreviate a company's name or title, you have to write out the whole name or title, first. You can't write *NASA*; you must write, *National Aeronautics Space Administration (NASA)*. Then, the next time NASA comes up, you can write the four letters only. It's simple.

No-no abbreviations. I'm going to put on my little white gloves and purse my lips and tell you that there are certain words that you certainly mustn't abbreviate. Such abbreviations are not *proper*. Ready? Here we go.

1. Stay away from abbreviating months, days, and holidays: No Mar., Mon., or X-mas allowed.
2. Keep a distance from abbreviated weights (lbs.), measures (tsp.), and states (SD or Fla.).
3. Make your orgs. full-length organizations, your corp. a full-length corporation, and your co. a full-length company.
4. And for heaven's sake, their names aren't "Wm." Or "Chas." Or "J." Their names are William, Charles, and John. Give the guys a break.

Dollar signs. Use the dollar sign when next to a large number (more than three words). Write it like this: $435. Otherwise, write out the word *dollar*, like this: Twenty dollar bill.

So there you have it: a listing of the silly and troubling issues, erroneous errors, and particularly picky problems jumping off the end of the professor's correction pen. Now you can avoid the red pen marks a wee bit more. Black and white is beautiful.

Chapter 25

Know the Number Details that Count
a.k.a. Special Number Knowledge

When it comes to academic writing, numbers are fabulous, dahling, just *fabulous!* Numbers are our friends. Numbers and statistics speak loudly, giving oomph to our key points. In fact, any time you can drop a specific number into your paper...*do* it. Words like *several, many,* and *some* are weak, so take the scrawny words out of the ring. We want the heavy-weight guys: numbers like one hundred, seven thousand, and ninety-six million.

Academic writers follow the number rules. Here, specially gathered together in one handy-dandy spot, you'll find number details that will raise your writer's number knowledge. There are nine separate number knowledge nuggets below. Dig in.

Nugget 1
When a number starts a sentence, spell it out. That's an easy rule to remember. *Forty-five individuals* start the sentence—not *45 individuals*. The phrase, *Three hundred species*, starts the sentence—not *300 species*. Start with a word.

Nugget 2
When you have two numbers side-by-side, write one as a numeral and one as a spelled out word. Twelve 49-ers played in the game. The child wrote 13 nines on the paper. Two different types of numbers, side-by-side, make the sentence easier to read.

Nugget 3
Spelling out numbers. Okay, here the rules get a little bit fuzzy. The *Associate Press* style guide tells us to spell out numbers that are from zero to nine (one, two, skip-a-few, nine); then, beginning with 10, you can use numerals.

But for the numbers ten and above, manuals disagree. The *Chicago Manual of Style* tells us to write out all numbers, from zero to ninety-nine (as I just did). Such differences make writing numbers complicated. Other sources tell us to write out numbers that are one or two words long, such as one, two, three...seventeen, twenty-six, eighty-four. (By the way, hyphenated numbers count as one word in word count, so hyphenated numbers are a bonus, when you're trying to stay within a word count for an assignment.)

With experts not able to make up their minds on what's right, what do we do? Choose your weapon—your particular style guide—and wield it. Always ask your instructor what he or she prefers. And at the very least, spell out the numbers zero through nine.

Nugget 4
Know the *keep numbers in their category* rule. If I started writing a number as a numeral, then I have to keep the *rest* of the numbers as numerals, when writing *in the same category*.

Here's an example: "The Excellento Company sold 34 widgets and 7 wodgets during the first six hours." Widgets and wodgets are in the same category, so we write numerals for both.

Do you see? Look back. Hours are different from widgets and wodgets, so I went back to writing *the word* six. Make sense? I know—picky, picky. Such are the rules of academic writing. I always say, if you struggle to remember these details, keep your style guide on hand and look up the rules when you need to.

Nugget 5
Decades. There are three ways to write decades. First, you can write 'em out: fifties and sixties. Second, you could write '50s and '60s.

But if you do write the numerals ('50s and '60s), make sure that your apostrophe comes before the number, not between the number and the "s."

Finally, you can write out the whole shebang: 1950s and 1960s. But again, steer clear of the apostrophe. The plain-ol' number will do.

Nugget 6
Centuries. Write 'em out: the nineteenth century. And I'm sure you noticed: no capitalization.

Nugget 7
Fractions. For simple fractions, write 'em out: It's one-third, one-half, and three-quarters. For mixed fractions, go ahead and write the numeral: 4 1/3, 12 1/2, and 45 3/4. For mixed fractions, Microsoft Word changes your fraction numeral into a done-for-you, nifty small package, like this: 12 ½ and 45 ¾. Cool.

Nugget 8

Percentages. In academia, most professors recommend that you write out the word, *percent*: Five percent…twenty percent…sixty-four percent. However, if you have a number that takes more than two words, such as one hundred seventy-five percent, then write out the numbers, next to the word: 175 percent.

Nugget 9

Ordinal numbers. Ordinal numbers include first, second, third, and so on. Don't write 1st, 2nd, 3rd, and so on. Write out the number word. Words rule.

Don't worry about memorizing all of the above. Keep the pages (and your weapon, I mean, style guide) handy. Then, when you need the number details, gather your number nuggets and write on.

EB Conroy, MA, MFA

SECTION 6

Grammar Follies:
Sticky Pairs and Staying Together

Chapter 26

One Is, Two Are
a.k.a. How Many, Present

Congratulations! **You've entered Section Six:** Grammar Follies and Sticky Pairs. Most of us consider grammar as fun as shoveling wet snow...or as fun as cleaning the shower...or as fun as picking burrs off your completely covered socks. The good news is that each sticky pair chapter is super short. Learn one at a time. And memorize them. You hafta-gotta-needta. Because...

Sticky pairs are words that absolutely have to go together. The pairs are attached at the hip; one never, ever, *ever* goes anywhere without the other. Our sticky pairs are like uniquely matched socks: Mixing and matching the socks is definitely not allowed. Learn the meaning behind the sticky pairs, and the most basic grammar points are in your pocket.

The first sticky pair answers the question, "So how many are there?" *One is* over here—and *two are* over there. *One is* in the bag—and *three are* in the bucket. *One is* the most reliable source—and *six more are* the next-most reliable sources. The sticky pair called *one is, two are* means that when you're writing about one thing, the one thing *is*. When writing about two or more things, the two *are*.

How is it that people mix up *how many* words? For example—how many times have you heard someone say, "The individuals is signed up for the class"? Ouch. The individuals are more than one, so we need to write, "The individuals (plural/more than one) *are*...." The right way to write the sentence is that the individual (singular/one) *is* signed up for the class.

Look at the list below and decide if you'd use *is* or *are*.
Terminal...Hmmmm...that would be, *the terminal is*. A terminal, whether a computer terminal or train terminal, *is* one place...and *one is*.

Corporation...that would be, *the corporation is*, because it's one corporation...and *one is*.

Scissors...that would be, *scissors are*. Oh my! How did THAT happen? I have one thing in my hand! Well, it's because scissors are called a PAIR of scissors. A pair is *more than one*...and more than one *are*.

I know: It's bizarre, but true. Now, to make things more complicated, I can say, *"The single* pair of scissors left on the table *is* broken"—because *one is*...but let's not go there (grammar torture isn't my goal). Let's stick with the *scissors are.*

Let's look at a group called *collective nouns.* A collective noun is a single word (noun) that stands for *more than one* (a group). Collective nouns are words that show a special class or group. Some common collective nouns include *family, flock, congregation,* and *team.* The trouble with collective nouns is that the single unit (group) is one...so the family is running late, the flock is flying high, the congregation is falling asleep, and the team is winning.

Then comes trouble. What if the family members are coming to dinner? Now we're talking about *members*—and members are *more than one*...hence, family members *are.* Again, we wouldn't say, "The *family are* coming to dinner" (incorrect). We say, "The family members are coming to dinner."

What if the team leaders are meeting together? We're talking about *leaders*— and leaders are *more than one*...hence, team leaders *are.* Again, we wouldn't say, "the *team are* meeting together" (incorrect). We say, "The *team leaders are* meeting together."

Make sense?

Now, to throw another strange ingredient into the mix—let's talk about the *one-were exception.* That's right. There is an exception. (I completely dislike those exceptions, don't you?)

Have you seen the famous Hollywood classic movie, *The Wizard of Oz?* In the Judy Garland version, the lion, standing inside of Oz with his companions, sings, "If I...were king...of the fore-e-e-e-e-e-st!"

Did you catch that? *If I were....* When wishing for something, you may—as a single entity—wish you were it, were there, or were whatever you want to be.

Go figure. It's an exception.

Simply remember: Single is and plural are.
One is; two are.
One is; more than one are.
A car is; two cars are.
A bird is; many birds are.
This one chapter is finished; many (if not all of you) are glad.

Chapter 27

One Was, Two Were
a.k.a. How Many, Past

Look at the title of this chapter, if you will. Does something sound kind-of familiar here? Last chapter, we talked about the sticky pair, *one is, two are.* Now we have another, quite similar sticky pair: *one was, two were.*

The second sticky pair answers the same question, *how many are there*? But this time, the answer is in past tense. If you have recollection of your grammar class many moons ago, you'll remember that *past tense* means that the action happened already. *One was* over here—and *two were* over there. *One was* in the bag—and *three were* in the bucket. *One was* the most reliable source—and *six more were* the next-most reliable sources.

The sticky pair called *one was, two were* means that when you're writing about one thing that happened already, the one thing *was*. When writing about two or more things that happened already, the two *were*.

I have a friend who frequently mixes up her *how many* words. For example, I'll hear my friend say, "Both girls was needing to be signed up for the class." Ouch. That hurt. I try not to let my friend see me cringe. Instead, I say back, "Ah, I agree—*both* girls *were* supposed to be signed up by today's deadline, *weren't* they?"

I truly believe that one of these days, my friend will get it. But it may take a while. You see, my friend has something working against her: Her parents didn't speak with *one was, two were* grammar. Whether we like it or not, while growing from wee sprouts into the semi-intelligent persons that we are today, we learn our sticky-pair grammar from the conversations spoken and observed with those closest to us.

Let's look again at that group, *collective nouns*. The same rules apply as were in the last chapter. Did you catch that? The rules—more than one rule—"as *were* in the last chapter." People typically don't speak like that last sentence, but the grammar is correct. Since a *family* is a single unit, the family *was*. Since *flock* is a single unit, the flock *was*. Since a *congregation* and a *team* are single units, then the congregation *was*…and the team *was*, too. However, once you put the congregation and team together, then they both *were*.

Hey—if your head's spinning, stop a sec and slowly read the last paragraph again. No worries. It'll come to you.

One more time: Single was and plural were.
One was; two were.
One was; more than one were.
A technician was; the technicians were.
The web site was; the web sites were.
This chapter was easy to comprehend; all of the chapters previous were easy, as well.

By the end of the book, you'll be a pro.

Chapter 28

It's Yours, You're Its
a.k.a. You Own it or it Owns You

Do you casually know a set of identical twins? I say *casually* because if you knew the two well, you'd be able to tell them apart. But when you know a set of twins in an informal way, you can easily get the two mixed up…which can be quite embarrassing.

Mixing up twins is exactly what happened to me. I have a friend with identical twin boys, Ben and Sam. I always saw the mom, but I didn't interact with the boys much. Growing up, the two boys had the same haircut, shared the same clothes, and (to my eyes) wore the same expressions on their faces. I always had to ask my kids, "Is that Ben or Sam?"

My daughter, best friends with the boys' sister, knew the boys extremely well. She looked at me with an incredulous look and bemoaned, "Mom! You've got to be kidding! You can't tell them apart?! *That's* Ben and *that's* Sam!" While she pointed, I grinned sheepishly. You'd think I'd learn to recognize the differences. But no matter how hard she tried to explain the boys' dissimilarity, my brain remained confused. I simply didn't hang around them that much.

Just like Ben and Sam, if you don't hang around and study them enough, similar-looking words can easily confuse us, too. The words *its* and *it's* have only an eentsy-weentsy apostrophe creating a difference between them. The same goes for *your* and *you're*. They look awfully close, to most of us.

But that apostrophe is a powerful dude. The minute he steps into the picture (or, shall I say, into the word), life changes dramatically for the sentence. The apostrophe creates a contraction: two words chopped and stuck together into one. *You have* becomes *you've*. *It will* becomes *it'll*. *Could not* becomes *couldn't*. Contractions are a wonderful way to write informally, and save space while you're at it.

So having an apostrophe in a contraction means that you can stretch the one word into two words, too (the opposite of what we did, above). *It's* becomes *it is*. *You're* becomes *you are*. *Haven't* becomes *have not*.

We don't use contractions in academic writing. We write the words out. But this is about words that look alike: its and it's, you're and your. Excuse my digression.

Here's the true test of whether you should put in an apostrophe and make a contraction: Elongate the word to its original two. If the words can become two, and the sentence still makes sense, then use the apostrophe.

So what's with the words that don't have an apostrophe? *Its* and *your* denote ownership. Here's an example sentence:

The dog ran into *its* doghouse.

The dog owns the house: *its doghouse*. So we don't use an apostrophe. Also, let's use the true test that we mentioned above: change the contraction back into two words and see if the sentence still makes sense.

The dog ran into *it is* dog house.

Nope. Putting in two words doesn't work—the sentence doesn't make sense. Therefore, we have proven that the sentence's use of *its* is a true case of ownership. And we don't use an apostrophe in our sentence about the dog.

Let's do the same for the word, *yours*. *Yours* denotes ownership. Here's an example sentence:

Your phone keeps ringing.

You own the phone, so we don't use an apostrophe. Let's try the true test again: Expand the single word into two words, and see if the sentence makes sense.

You are phone keeps ringing.

Nope. Putting in two words doesn't work—the sentence doesn't make sense. Therefore, we have proven that the sentence's use of *your* is a true case of ownership. So we don't use an apostrophe.

Ownership = no apostrophe
Contractions that can expand to two words = yes apostrophe

It's like knowing the difference between twins. The difference is oh-so slight—and oh, so important. Don't get caught like I did with Ben and Sam.

Get to know these sticky pairs well, so that you can quickly tell them apart.

You're its, it's yours. You are its, it is yours.

No worries. You're going to get **its** simplicity. And **it's** a fact: **Your** writing will become better, every day.

Chapter 29

They're over There with Their Grammar Book
a.k.a. Contraction, Point, and Own It

Now we come to the triplets—three words that sound alike but are also easily confused: *they're, there,* and *their.* Hence, we have another sticky pair (or, actually, trio) to remember. Let's look at the easy way to keep the three straight.

First, the word, *they're,* is a contraction. That means that you can expand the one word into two words, *they* and *are.* If you're writing and can use the two words instead of the one, then you're ready to go with *they're.*

> **They're** in the rocket ship. **They are** in the rocket ship. Yes, it works.

Second, the word, *there,* stands for a place. I can point to *there. There* it is. It is *there.* If you're pointing (actually, someone—or something—in your text is pointing), then you're ready to go with *there. There* is often followed by *is* in the phrase, *there is.* And *there* can be followed by *are,* as in *there are. There will be, there has been, there had been, there could be, should be,* and *would be*…they're all *to-be* verb forms that you'll find stuck onto the word, *there.*

Here are example sentences using the word *there* correctly:

*The senator believes that **there is** one answer to the problem. **There are** three additional leaders who vehemently disagreed. When all four people went over **there** to the conference room to get coffee, a fight ensued.*

Remember the word, *there,* as so: We have a ***there is,*** a ***there are*** (or any verb form of to-be), and the point-at-it-version of ***there***—all standing for a place. *There* is an actual, physical spot on the earth—or a mental spot in our brain. (I know you can't see me right now. But imagine me pointing as I say, "Something is ***there*….")

Finally, the word *their* means *ownership*. *Their* is actually more related to ***its*** and ***your*** (from the last chapter) than anything else—because *their* is also an ownership word. Let's take a look at some examples of the word *their* in action.

Bob and Sue went to **their** *house. They own the house. The house is* **theirs.** *Therefore, the use is correct and the sentence works.*

Their *plans were thwarted by the pirates. They own the plans. The plans are* **theirs.** *So again, the use is correct and the sentence works.*

The ballet was the perfect choice for the program, as the performance demonstrated **their** *abilities well. They have the abilities. The abilities are* **theirs.** *Once again, the use is correct and the sentence works.*

Now here's something interesting about the triplets: We try not to use any of the triplets much in academic writing. That's right. In academic writing, *they're, there,* and *there* are words to avoid.

Let me tell you why.

First, *they're* is a contraction. In academic writing, we avoid contractions, because contractions are informal. Nix the word **they're** and write out **they are.**

Next, the pointing kind of *there* is out because the word raises questions. It's a word that makes the reader ask, *Uh…where?* As writers, we don't want the reader to pause. We don't want the reader to have to double-check what he or she just read. Anything that makes the reader pause and double check is absolutely, positively *not* desirable.

There are actually five pointing words that make a reader ask questions: *this, these, those, that,* and *there.* We covered the first four pointing words in Chapter 1.

If you write *this,* the reader asks, *Uh…what is the writer referring to? What is "this"?*

If you write *these* or *those,* the reader asks, *Uh…what is the writer referring to, with the words, these or those? These what? Those what?*

If you write *that* in the pointing sense of the word, the reader asks, *Uh… what is the writer referring to? What is "that"?*

If you write the word *there* in a pointing sense of the word, the reader asks, *Uh…where is "there"?* Question words hold up the reader's thoughts, keeping the reader from moving forward smoothly. Therefore, pointing words should be avoided.

Finally, the word *their* is an ambiguous pronoun. (Please tell me you remember all about avoiding ambiguous pronouns! Yes…thank you.) We can almost always write a sentence without a pronoun.

The word *their* is a word that can be dropped right off the page, with little or no impact on the sentence—except to make the remaining sentence clear, concise, and bunches better than it was before. Okay, so my prejudice is coming through a bit. Let me show you why….

Here is an example sentence where the word *their* can be zapped quite easily:

*The candidates wanted to spend **their** constituents' money on print advertising, but **their** funding ran dry after the television ads' production.*

Now…watch the magic as *their* disappears….

The candidates wanted to spend constituents' money on print advertising, but funding ran dry after the television advertisements' production.

Ooh-lah-lah! Gone—with no negative impact! In fact…the sentence is more concise, direct, and clean. *That's* the kind of writing we want in college.

One last word: Students always say to me, *Can't I use "there" or "their" once in a while? After all, I see professional writers do it.* My answer is simple: Yes, professional writers use such words. And, yes, you can use the words. (I'm not going to come to your house and tie your hands so that you can't use the keyboard.)

Buuuuuut…(that's a big "but")—Use the words, and your writing clouds up into fuzzy meanings. Each little wee-bitty-faux pas adds up, until your reader says, *I don't like what I'm reading. Something about the words and sentences isn't right. Reading the piece simply doesn't feel good.* Readers may not be able to identify exactly *what* they don't like…but they'll know that *something* is off. Something on the page takes your work down a rung or two on the reader's ladder of understanding and admiration.

So I have a question for you: Is it worth the risk, to lower the dynamics of your written piece and possibly have your reader feel negative about your writing? I hope you're saying, *no*. Because it's my firm belief that, when it comes to writing, you should shoot for the target's bull's-eye at all times.

Make a decision: Use the hints and helps in the book that you're reading right now. **They're** bound to add up. The positives found **there** in your writing will get into your writing. And your audience will enjoy **their** reading experience much, much more.

Chapter 30

Bigger Than, Maybe Then
a.k.a. Comparing Versus Timing

One letter can make a huge difference. Change a letter, and the word *spin* becomes *spit*. If you spit on the playground equipment, you'll get into a whole lot more trouble than if you spin on it. Spices become spaces. Put spaces in the recipe, instead of spices, and cooking turns into a long event. Shops become shoes. A row of shops takes up a whole lot more space than a row of shoes, doesn't it? See what I mean? When it comes to the meaning of a word, one little letter can pick a pinch. I mean, pack a punch.

Than and ***then*** **only have one letter's difference.** But that little vowel adjustment drastically changes the meaning of the word.

Than (with an "a") is a comparing word. The roller coaster hill was **bigger than** I first thought. The dinner plate has **more** on it **than** I can eat. The grilled kabobs are **better than** I could have imagined. I can be **happier than** I was yesterday, **warmer than** I was last December, **healthier than** I was last week, and **smarter than** I was a year ago.

Notice the /er/ words that can come before the word *than* (bigger, better, happier, warmer, healthier, and smarter). *Than* attracts /er/ words. If you have comparison (something-#1 is more than something-#2), then use *than*.

Then (with an "e") is a cohort to "if." In academic writing the bosom buddies of *if-then* actually stick together at all times. Remember it: *If—then*. If I go on the roller coaster after eating lunch, **then** I may regret the choice later. **If** I eat all that's on the dinner plate, **then** I'll not need to eat again until breakfast. **If** I wear a warm coat, **then** I probably won't get cold when ice skating with my friends. **If** and **then** are inseparable, making the words a sticky pair to remember.

Another point of interest: *Then* hangs with *when and after*. **When** X happens, **then** Y happens. **After** A happens, **then** B will happen. Timing words of a feather flock together.

And let's not forget *and,* as used in speaking. *And* makes *then* even stronger: **And then** the princess kissed the frog. **And then** the frog turned into a prince. **And then** the two lived happily ever after. Not really. But in the child's mind, excitement reigns…and ***and then*** becomes the connecting phrase that builds excitement.

However, in academic writing, do not, not, not use *and then*. Ever. Save it for kid conversations.

***Then* is what I call a *timing word*.** *Then* handles the passing of time. *Then* shows the reader a *causal relationship*—fancy words that simply mean a change takes place in the second factor, based on something that went on with the first factor.

If you apply what you learn in the course, **then** you will become a better writer.
If you stay up too late, **then** your eyelids will have a hard time staying open tomorrow.
And **if** you get to the end of the chapter and find that it was shorter than you first thought, **then** you are welcome to jump up and down and shout, "Hallelujah!" (It's **more** fun **than** sitting there, expressionless, isn't it?)

Chapter 31

Not Only, But Also
a.k.a. All Four Words, Please

Are you ready for one of the shortest chapters in the book? Here's a sticky pair that's easy to remember.

If you write *not only*, you must follow with the words *but also*. Really. Every time. No exceptions.

Not only **is a no-change pair.** The two words are always in the same order, as though one word: *not only*.

The second two words, *but also*, are more adventurous. They aren't afraid to move away from each other in the sentence...even if it's just a wee bit.

Here are a few correct sentences with our sticky pair:
Not only *did the dog jump the fence,* **but also** *he decided to run into the neighbor's yard.*

Or, with a little adventuresome space in *but also*....
Not only *did the dog jump the fence,* **but** *then he* **also** *decided to run into the neighbor's yard.*

Here's one more example:
Not only *did the professor write a short chapter,* **but also** *she decided to be a bit silly with the words at the end.*

Or, with the *but also* spread out a bit....
Not only *did the professor write a short chapter,* **but** *she* **also** *decided to be a bit silly with the words at the end.*

And there you have it.

Chapter 32

May I? If You Can…
a.k.a. Permission or Possibility

Are you being polite, or are you truly asking me if it's possible? With writing the sticky pair *may I* or *can I*, the two distinctions are important.

May I **asks permission.** *May I* open the door for you? *May I* begin the assignment early? *May I* write on a topic that has to do with history, as opposed to one that has to do with a current governmental issue?

May I is a polite request, a deferential move showing courteous respect. (*May I* is fancy for *pretty-please.*)

Can I **asks if I'm capable—or if it's physically possible, without consequences.** *Can I* make the cake with rolled oats added, or will it ruin the consistency of the whole thing? *Can I* add the program to my computer, or will it cause problems with the operating system? *Can I* fit all of the DVDs into the cabinet, or will I need to buy a bigger cabinet?

In each case of *can I,* **the question is** *not* **whether it's okay to do so;** the question is, *is it physically possible?*

Neither *can I* **or** *may I* **is used much in academic writing.** If you're writing about whether or not a country *can* use a chemical on crops, you'll need to change your words to say whether or not they will ***decide to*** use the chemical. Because the people *can* physically take the chemical, put it into the machine, and disperse it over the plants. The question is not in their physical capability; it's in the decision making.

There are lots of things that we *can* **do.** However, if you are inquiring as to the social acceptability of an action (you're asking permission), then it's ***may.*** If you are asking whether an action is best (if you should or shouldn't do something), then write ***may.***

If asking whether or not there is a physical ability for an event to come about, then write *can.*

Can I end writing the chapter now? Yes, I physically can. *May* I do so? I imagine you're saying *yes*, so...on with it.

Chapter 33

Keep Tense!
a.k.a. Freeze! Stay Where You Are!

Have you ever been around hyperactive people who can't sit still? Like a dizzy fly trying to get out of a tight space, they flit, dive bomb, and jiggle-jaggle all over. You want to say, "Hey! Stop it! Calm down and settle in, puhleeze!"

Some of us write our sentences using *tense* like dizzy flies. *Tense* refers to when the action happens: in the past (past tense), present (present tense), or future (future tense). The dizzy-fly writer jumps from past, to present, back to past, up to future, back to past. He's not only bonking his head on the ceiling of what's acceptable in writing, but he's also smashing right through, making holes in the ceiling where rain, sleet, and snow can pour in.

Let me show you what a dizzy-fly writer's sentence looks like.

She is in the garage cleaning for an hour, and she thought the place will be looking great because she was doing a fantastic job.

Oh. Boy. Where are we, in time—the past, the present, or the future?

Here's the analysis:
First, our young lady *is* in the garage (present tense);
then she **thought** (past tense)
that the place **will be** (future tense)
looking great because she **was** (past tense)
doing a fantastic job.

Hold your ears while I take a moment to scream. There. I feel better. Now, I'm able to look you square in the eye and say…

Stop jumping between past, present, and future. Freeze! Stay where you are, okay? If you're writing in past tense—where events already happened— then stay in the past. That means it *did* happen, *was* finished, *had been* doing its thing, and any past-tense word or words with an "ed" ending (like I scream**ed**, **tore** my hair out, and sigh**ed** a minute ago).

If you're in the present, stay in the present. Stay with *inging*—my way of saying that you need to write present tense words with *ing*: sing**ing**, swing**ing**, and bring**ing** your writing into control.

In the present, you're also directly involved: I sing; I swing; I bring.

Finally, if you're writing in the future, you *will* be doing something. In a paper, we may write that a company president states that he will be making significant changes to organizational policy. Ahem. That's *will be*. If he *will be*, then stay with his future status, while on that topic. The *present perfect tense*—using **has** been or **have** been—may creep in, too...and if so, stick with it.

When taking standardized English tests, it's important to know the time-sensitive words we're talking about. Standardized test writers create sentences with lists of three items. Those pesky test makers will try to fool you with time-travel errors by mixing up the *verb tense* between the three items in the list. You won't be fooled, though.

You'll know how to identify the sentence with all of the action happening in the same time zone. Past stays in the past. Present stays in the present. And future stays in the future.

When writing long sentences in college-level papers, don't forget where you are; keep tense. Read what you wrote carefully, with an eye for those past-present-future words.

I have a word picture for you that will help you never to forget to pay attention to tense: Picture in your mind the grammar police standing in a crouched position, two hands on the outstretched gun, which is pointed at your paper: **Freeze! Stay where you are!**

Don't make them shoot your paper.

SECTION 7

Structure & Form:
The Art & Rhythm of the Whole-Enchilada Paper

Section 7 moves us into how to begin the craft of writing dynamic
essays and papers.
The next book in the *Simplified Writing* series, *Simplified Research Writing*,
more fully explores, explains, and simplifies the mystique around
writing essays, papers, and longer works.
This is an introduction.
Enjoy.

Chapter 34

Narrow Your Topic
a.k.a. Use Baby Bear's Size Chart

It's time to write an essay or paper. Okay, promise me you won't freak out. Because most of us get longer writing assignments assigned and we freak out. (*Oh no! I have to write a PAPER!*) You write good sentences. You can sculpt a paragraph. You can even hook those paragraphs together. Once you have your topic, there's a process to follow. And, as always, the process makes life easier.

Your teacher or professor either decides what you're going to write about in your essay paper, or you'll be able to choose. If your topic is assigned, simply accept the assignment and go with it. Being befuddled or brazenly unhappy does no one good (and wastes time). Grin and move on. If you're allowed to choose your topic, think of the experience as a way to learn a ton about something that interests you.

Seriously. Take advantage of the opportunity to delve into happy learning moments.

I believe that you should love your paper's topic. After all, you're going to be spending a great amount of time together. A good relationship together is much easier to bear than having to fight your way through an entire paper with a topic you dislike.

Your topic also needs to be the right size. As in the story of *The Three Bears*, your topic can be too big, too small, or just right.

A too-big topic quickly gets out of control. There's so much information available on your topic, you could easily write a book.

A too-small topic becomes a frustrating exercise of trying to squeeze a gallon of orange juice out of one orange. You've picked a topic so small, you can't find enough information to write on.

The just right topic is the best, just as in Goldilocks' bowl, chair, and bed's just-right perfection. Rarely do we have a non-Goldilocks moment, when we begin the decision-making process for topic choosing. (We. Will. Have. To. Think. And. Then. Choose.) Know it and go with it.

In other words, don't get bent out of shape when you get out your binoculars and start searching for the best topic to write on. Know that it's a process, to find what you're looking for and focus in. Zeroing in on your topic takes thought. And that thinking can actually be fun—because playing with ideas (not committing to an idea until you've rolled it around in your hands and tossed it into the air a bit) *is* fun…if you decide it is.

The tendency is to choose a topic that's too broad. For instance, the topic *Italian food* can turn into fifty books' worth of information. *Italian breads* is a topic size that's more manageable…and better yet, *Italian Bread Making Practices Today* or *Pastries Originating in Italy* are more manageable topics bringing *focus and specificity* to the paper that your teacher or professor will love.

The last paragraph shows how to narrow a topic into a Goldilocks-sized product. To narrow your topic, slice it down to the next size. Simply ask yourself, *what is a smaller, more manageable idea that stems from my original idea?* Keep moving smaller until you get to the Goldilocks-sized topic.

Try it.

Chapter 35

Make Your Research Question "Just Right"
a.k.a. Puny and Giganto Don't Work

To research is to find and get information. Research means to simply go out and get ideas from others. And, before we go out and get, we must know what we're looking for. To find what we're looking for, we have to know the question we're asking.

What am I trying to find out in my paper, anyhoo?

From *what is the meaning of life* to *what should I eat for breakfast,* life is full of questions. Yes, your research paper has questions, too (go figure). Your research question is the over-arching query that you're seeking to answer, by writing your paper.

Research questions come in three sizes: puny, giganto, and just right (yes, we're back to Goldilocks again). Puny research questions don't cover enough of the idea.

A puny question might be, "What is the date of the first manned space flight?" The reason the question is too puny is that the answer is so short and direct, there's no way you could write a paper on the answer to the question.

On the other side of the teeter totter, a giganto Research Question on the same topic might be, "What were the historical circumstances that influenced and led to the first manned space flight?" What makes the question giganto is that you could go back to the history of flight in general, which can encompass years and years. You could go back further to include the ideas and influences of artists, scientists, and thinkers' who dreamed of space flight. And since the term *history* can encompass all of time (did Adam and Eve watch the pterodactyl and dream of flight?), we're back to the place of writing books instead of papers. Waaaaaayyy too big.

Let's try another example.

What if my supposed research question was, "In the 1980s, what event changed the face of Deaf Education on college campuses?" Since the question evokes a single final answer, the question is too small. (The event was the Deaf President Now protest on the Gallaudet University campus in

March of 1988, leading to the appointment of the first deaf president of the school.)

A too-big question might be, "What were college campuses like in the United States in the 1980s?" All campuses? Are we talking about all of the years in the '80s? If so, get ready to write the book again.

A more appropriate question might be, "What cultural factors led to the Deaf President Now protest in 1988?" The simple phrase, *cultural factors*, changes the game and makes the question one that's *just right* for writing a paper.

One more time: Let's find a research question for an argumentative paper. Hmmm…how about the topic of immunizations for children?

A too-small research question might be, "What is the name of the researcher who developed the Polio vaccine?" (It's not really an argumentative question because there's nothing arguable here.) The answer to the question is puny. So the question is puny.

What about a new question: "What are the worst diseases of childhood?" (It's an argumentative question because some may argue what constitutes *the worst*.) The answer is giganto, so the question is giganto.

Finally, let's craft a just-right research question: "Should toddlers be given Measles-Mumps-Rubella (MMR) vaccinations?" The question is just right because we're talking about toddlers (as opposed to all children) and only one vaccine (MMR). You can now fill a paper with the right amount of information, to make the paper a reasonable size.

Finding the just right Research question size is important. The size of the question cuts you off early (the puny question), gives you a feeling of endless, bottomless writing (the giganto question), or lets you feel like the job at hand is doable (the *just right* question).

When it comes to finding the right sized research question, don't go with your first idea. Play with the possibilities. Don't settle for less. Settle into the best.[11]

---

[11] Again, a shameless plug (because it's *good* for you): The *Simplified Research Writing* book will be your best research writing helper and friend. Get it. On Amazon. Today. Okay? Thanks.

Chapter 36

It's a Simple Four Step Dance
a.k.a. Plan, Draft, Revise, and Edit…in that Order

W**riting a paper is like learning a dance with four simple steps.** Follow the Four Step Dance, and the paper performs for you.

STEP ONE: PLAN
Planning **isn't the same as** *thinking*. *Thinking* can be sitting down and staring at the ceiling while sipping cocoa, waiting for your brain cogs to click, engage, and interlock into a brilliant "Aha!" moment.

Brilliant "Aha!" moments rarely happen without a push. We have to make sure we have the right cogs moving. The push is *the plan*.

Planning begins with a viable topic. We need an idea that not only works but is also a *good* idea. Like blowing bubbles out of a little stick with a circle on the end, ideas can float all about our heads like pretty little things.

So always make sure that your topic fits the assignment. Don't guess; check with your instructor. And if you have freedom to choose a topic, make sure that you fully understand the intent—or purpose—of the paper. (Re-read the previous chapter.)

While planning, set your direction—that means knowing what to include in your paper. Find direction, also known as the *order and scope* of what you're going to cover, by developing your content *before you write one single word of the text.*

There are many proven methods of coming up with ideas for content. To crank up the momentum of your brain machinery and plan your paper, here are a few proven methods to get the job done:

Free Writing
Free-writing means writing down everything that bubbles to the surface of your thoughts about the topic. In free writing, to think is to write. Through writing anything and everything related to the topic, you're able to identify viable ideas. Free writing isn't a group activity; it's best completed on your

own.

Clustering (a.k.a. Balloons or Webbing)

For all you artsy doodlers out there, clustering is for you. Start clustering by drawing a balloon-shaped circle (or box, or hexagon, or whatever shape you like) in the center of the page. Inside the shape, write the topic (central idea).

Next, draw at least three shapes (for example, three new bubbles) floating around the outside central shape (the big middle bubble).

Now fill each of the three outside shapes with the main categories that make up your idea.

When you have the main categories that make up your main idea, connect the three outside ideas to the main idea with lines (like a giant connect-the-dots game).

Now you get to multiply your three bubbles. For each of the three ideas, create subcategories (three shapes around each shape).

Do you see it? Our bubbles had babies. (!)

We're building out by threes. Here's another way to draw it:

Each shape spawns new ideas or subcategories. For clustering, you can work with one other person or a group.

Brainstorming

Most of us have heard of brainstorming—that whoop-dee-doo free-for-all where you write anything down about your topic that comes to mind. But you can't be too whoop-dee-doo about it, mind you (or you're into free writing).

Begin by focusing your thoughts with one sentence about your subject. Then write everything you can think about on the subject. Answer Who-What-When-Where-Why-How (WWWWWH) questions, to make sure that you've covered a broad range of possibilities for your paper's direction.

Patterns should emerge from your thinking—pieces of linear *this-should-come-first-and-that-should-come-next* ideas. You're on your way to arranging the content of your paper. You can brainstorm alone, as a partner, or with a group.

Listing

Listing is…um…well, it's making a list. Write ideas, phrases, and statements about your topic in a list. (Listing is a concept that's as uncomplicated as it can get.) Simply write ideas without subtopics. You'll be able to break your ideas into similar groups or subgroups later. Write all that you know about your topic, as ideas flow in general categories. You can easily move your list of statements into an outline, if you'd like. You can list alone, with a best buddy, or with friends.

Questions

To complete the planning stage through questions, all you need to do is pretend to be an interviewer. Again, the WWWWWH questions pop up as main titles on your page. Then simply fill in the answers. The difference between basic brainstorming and brainstorming with the WWWWWH questions is that with questions, you won't get side tracked and deviate to any old idea (something that's permissible in brainstorming). Questioning should stay in strict format. You can ask questions to yourself, or another person can ask you questions.

Trees

Trees are my favorite way of idea making. Much like clustering, you create a picture of a tree trunk with branches as a visual diagram of your paper's ideas.

To create a tree, draw a trunk; write the main topic inside (on) the trunk.

Next, draw at least three branches extending upwards from the trunk; then write your three main areas to cover in the paper, within the branches.

From each main idea branch, draw three more branches extending upward; the new upward branches are divisions—new ideas extending, dividing, and expanding into branchy subtopics.

Feel free to extend a branch as many times as possible. The goal is to land on a branch covering a single topic that will nicely fill one paragraph.

When your tree has a good amount of branches, order the branches in 1-2-3 order, for your paper content. Then re-draw your branches in the new order, ordering information where each paragraph logically moves to the next.

Then all a writer has to do is moving across the branches of the tree in order, writing paragraphs on each branch's topic. You can create a tree by yourself or with others.

By the way, half of your total time spent creating your paper should be in Step One. It's true. HALF. The point is, if you plan well, you don't have to think too hard, to write. It's all laid out for you. Follow your ideas in order, and your paper will flow. So take the time to Plan.

STEP TWO: DRAFT

Once you've hammered out a plan, it's time to draft. I commonly refer to drafting as *spitting it out*. To draft is to write. Not revise. Not edit. (We'll talk about those in a second.)

Using the info from planning, begin writing. Write in logical order, from the ideas that you already lined up in brainstorming.

Here's what most people do, for drafting: Most people want to write a sentence, back space and delete, write again, then write half of a new sentence, then go back and change a word, then write the second half of the sentence, then back space and take out the first sentence, then add two more sentences, then go back and change a word in the third sentence, then change the order…*pant, pant, pant*…S – T – O – P…STOP THAT!!!

(* Wipes sweat from brow, takes a deep breath, lets it out, stares at you right between the eyes)

THAT is NOT drafting! (It's more like spasmodic seizures.) Sit still and keep writing. No matter what, write and don't stop. *Draft* it out. Don't hiccup, spin, turn, or spasmodically spit out the kind of writing that masquerades as drafting.

Then…

STEP THREE: REVISE

Revise your draft. Revising is all about moving large pieces around. To revise is to move a whole section, paragraph, or line. It's also about flipping the order of the words in a sentence.

Most times, we write our sentences like we think and talk: We place the most important ideas at the beginning of our sentences. And afterthought ideas end up pinned on the end of the sentence. That's. Not. Good.

To engage the reader, we need do the exact opposite. Place the most important information *at the end of each sentence.* Seriously. Switch your sentence content around.

Here's an example. I might write the following in my first draft: *Seating at square tables causes more emotional separation of participants, even though individuals tend to avoid round tables because of forced interaction.* But that first-scribbled sentence isn't strong. It's garbled and doesn't make much sense. The sentence arrangement is long and not the strongest set up for clarity.

No worries. You got the ideas down on the paper. That's all that mattered. Now, during the revision step, we get to play with the content, to make our point.

This arrangement is stronger: *Individuals tend to avoid sitting at round tables because the arrangement forces interaction. Square table seating causes emotional separation from participants, as well.*

Ha! Wonderful! We took the draft and revised the ideas, for clarity. Revising is the correct place to make completely appropriate flips, flops, and movements of text.

STEP FOUR: EDIT
NOW you can edit. To edit...
* Check your punctuation, capitalization, and grammar.
* Take out all of The No-No List words that snuck in when your back was turned.
* Pull out your gun and shoot the pronouns off your paper, replacing the pronouns with specific nouns.
* Stick the subject smack-dab-up next to the action verb, effectively turning the passive phrases into active ones.
* Make sure that there are no slip-ups in the format.
* Clear the air of all the itsy-bitsy bothersome and unnecessary details, and leave the reader with a blue-sky paper to enjoy.

Be sure to write your paper in One-Two-Three-Four order. Don't mix up the order of the Four-Step Dance—because mix-ups increase frustration and take away precious time. You don't want to do that. Follow the steps.

Chapter 37

Build a Traditional Outline
a.k.a. It's Nice to Have a Home Base

Somewhere along the line, you'll most likely need to use a traditional outline. I believe outlines are the best way to hone in on key information, to write the cleanest, most sense-making essay or paper. An outline helps to put your ideas in order. And an outline helps you stay on track, when drafting your work.

In order to write an outline, you need to know the main points of your paper. Then you need to know the sub points that sit under the main points. Finally, you'll need to discover the sub-sub points that sit under the sub points. Everything multiplies outward. Each point is broken down and sifted out into smaller points. Or think of your outline as an expanding root system.

When is the best time to create an outline? Because outlines are all about taking ideas and making them line up, ready to march onto your paper, your outline is best created *after* brainstorming and *before* drafting.

Outlines are organized with letters and numbers. I'm going to show you the most basic, traditional outline that you can use. I call it the traditional, or home base, outline.

With traditional outlines, there are a few guidelines to always follow. First, use Roman numerals for the main points. Sub points are organized with capital letters (A, B, C), and sub-sub points are organized with numbers (1, 2, 3). Finally, if your outline has a ton of information, you may even get to use lower case letters (a, b, c) and itsy-bitsy lower case letters in mini Roman numerals (i, ii, iii, iv, v).

Another guideline: Outlines must always have more than one division of an idea. If you have an A, then you must also have a B. If you have a 1, then you must also have a 2. And so on. That's the way it goes. (Don't ask me why, because I don't know, and I don't really want to break out into the song, *Tradition!* from *Fiddler on the Roof.*)

The top of your outline begins with the Roman numeral I. The introduction is always I. Easy. Your instructor will probably want you to write your thesis statement under the I...and maybe even put the hook in there, too. It will look like this:

I. Introduction
Hook: blah, blah, blah
Thesis statement: blah, blah, blah

The next part of the outline is the Roman numeral II. Your first real point of your paper (first main section) is written out after the II...after section I...like so:

I. Introduction
Hook: blah, blah, blah
Thesis statement: blah, blah, blah

II. First Main Point (not a sentence, but a phrase)

And under the main point, check out the next items:

II. First Main Point
      A. Sub point
      B. Sub point

And if you have sub-sub points, look how fancy you can get:

I. Introduction
Hook: blah, blah, blah
Thesis statement: blah, blah, blah

II. First Main Point
      A. Sub point
            1. sub-sub point
            2. sub-sub point (notice, sub point A has to have a 2, because it has a 1)
      B. Sub point
            1. sub-sub point 1
                  a. sub-sub-sub point (this is getting fun)
                  b. sub-sub-sub point
            2. sub-sub point 2
                  a. sub-sub-sub point of #2
                  b. sub-sub-sub point number two of #2
                        i. super-sub point (!)
                        ii. another super-sub point (yee-haw!)

     c. sub-sub-sub point extra
  C. Sub point (the last sub point for the first section of the paper)
     1. sub-sub point 1 (you'd want to have one of these, to
     balance A and B's size)
     2. sub-sub point 2

III. Second Main Point (second section of the paper)
  A. Sub point numero uno, under the Second Main Point
     1. sub-sub point
     2. sub-sub point…etc. etc. etc. (Now I break into verse from
     The King and I, "Etcetera, Etcetera, Etcetera!")

And on we go, until we've listed all of the main points of the paper. In the example above we'll most likely want a Roman numeral IV, so that there are three sections in the body of our paper. Then the last Roman numeral is the conclusion…as so:

V. Conclusion

The conclusion is the *So What?* Always leave the reader with an answer to the *So What?* (More on that in an upcoming chapter).

In the outline, we'll most likely NOT write a concluding idea, because, hey, we've not written the paper yet. We may not really know the most important concluding idea until the research and writing is complete.

Frankly, your initial (supposed) conclusion idea (when you write your outline) may not stick around, when you get to the end. That's okay. Your conclusion will have a better chance of finding you after you've completed the first draft.

Outlines exist in a strange dichotomy: First, outlines are meant to be followed. They keep us on track. But also, outlines can be re-envisioned, rearranged, reworked.

When writing, we'll most likely find new information that wasn't in our Step One planning. That's okay. Be smart, be alert, and be flexible enough to realize a good outline change when it comes up and bites you on the nose.

And that, my friend, is what we need to know about outlines.

Chapter 38

Make Your Thesis Complete
a.k.a. It's Time to Blueprint

Good thesis statements rock…because they're so full of great content, with great purpose power, to propel your reader into your ideas. But thesis statements can also be tough to wrap our minds around…because they have so much to do in their little lifetimes.

Effective thesis statements are clear, persuasive, state a position, and anticipate support for the position. I have a ton of information about crafting a great thesis statement that you'll find in the *Simplified Research Writing* book.

Know this: Your thesis statement is ONE sentence that tells the reader what your paper is about. And if all you had in your little hand was the thesis statement, with no wand-waving whatsoever, you'd be able to know exactly what the entire essay or paper was about. Boom.

For time's sake, let's savor three elements that spice up your thesis statement: the *time-bound element*, the *geographically-bound element*, and the technique of *blueprinting*.

#1 – The Time-bound Element

A time-bound element tells the reader *when*. Time-bound words include *today*, *within the last twenty years* (or *century*…or *five hundred years*…pick a time), and *in the future*. Time-bound elements bring specificity that moves your topic from *giganto* to *reasonably sized*.

In my opinion, time bound elements should be in every single thesis statement.

#2 – The Geographically-bound Element

A geographically-bound element tells the reader *where*. Geographically-bound words include *in Europe*, *in the United States*, *on the African continent*, and *globally*. Time-bound elements also bring specificity, pulling your topic into the *reasonably sized* category.

And, for that reason, geographically-bound elements should be in every single thesis statement. (Do you see a pattern here?)

#3 – The Qualification

When you're writing to make a point, your topic will have two sides. It's no secret: We all believe that *our* side is the *best* side to be on. Your thesis statement will tell what side you believe in, simply by asserting what your paper is all about. You put your beliefs out there, for all to see (in your paper)—telling why *your side is best*, right?

But when you *admit that you know at least one of the other side's points,* something magical happens. And I'm going to show you why that magic needs to be in your thesis.

Here's where your magical *"although statement"* comes in. I can best illustrate what I mean by an example. Watch.

Here's an argumentative thesis statement:
German Shepherd dogs are excellent guard dogs and family companions, making the breed one of the best choices for families living in rural areas.

The sentence made a claim: Because of two qualities—guarding and companionship--German Shepherds are "best" for rural families. What's the first thing a Mastiff or Collie lover will say? *No, our breed is better!*

By addressing the "other side," I can make the thesis stronger by pointing out that there are other cool breeds, too. How? By adding the *although statement.*

Although there are a number of breeds with skills as farm dogs, German Shepherd dogs are excellent guard dogs and family companions, making the breed one of the best choices for families living in rural areas.

The "although statement" is officially called a *qualification.* (I call the qualification the "although statement" because we use the word *although* at the beginning of the qualifying phrase. And it's easy to remember.)

Now stay with me here. This isn't hard. And it's powerful.

To *qualify an argument* is to add more information or evidence. The added information and evidence makes your statement more specific. When you make your thesis more specific, using the other side's "first argument" welling up in their mind (often with raging waves of an angry sea), the qualification takes away some of the opposition's edge.

We'll discuss the amazing qualification in depth, in the Simplified Research Writing book. For now, simply know:

If you want a super-strong thesis statement, add a qualification.

#4 – The Blueprint

To *blueprint* is to give away your paper's main ideas for free. Blueprinting is a specific, doable concept helping a paper's thesis statement come alive.

To blueprint your thesis, you must place *the main points*—the keywords or key phrases—of your essay/paper into your thesis statement. Let me show you some examples.

Because of Google and search engines, we know all about keywords and key phrases. To take an idea and boil it down to a *keyword* is to nail down the most important, overarching *single word* that gets your idea across. To sculpt a *key phrase* is to find the most important *two or few words* that get your main idea across.

You need keywords or key phrases, to make your blueprinted thesis statement work.

Here are thesis statements employing the amazingly-cool blueprinting strategy:

Example 1: European youth centers in urban areas today help to create a safe place for young people to learn the value of community, responsibility, and education.

The three major areas or sections of the paper are *the community, responsibility,* and *education*…and notice the time-bound element—*today*—and the geographically-bound element—*European.*

Example 2: Although non-profit organizations' mission and vision statements, goals and objectives, and best practices have been influenced by leadership theory over the last four decades, non-profit groups in America have yet to take advantage of the full scope of the current body of leadership knowledge available today.

The paper will touch on *the mission and vision statements, goals and objectives,* and *best practices*—and show that there's more very-cool-and-amazing leadership information out there, that will help non-profit groups succeed. Oh yes, and notice the time-bound element—*over the last four decades*—and the geographically-bound element—*in America.* "All present and accounted for, Captain!" *salute

Example 3: Despite the fact that today's experts may promote the use of popular educational Smart Phone, iPod, and iPad gaming applications as beneficial to a child's performance in school, applications in the form of games lead to shorter attention spans and an unrealistic view of life, thereby causing children who use applications to perform more poorly in school than their counterparts who do not.

Okay, now follow me on this one; it's long but amazing. The paper will cover the major areas of…
1. Opposing beliefs about applications (the purported benefits of application gaming for children)
2. A claim regarding shorter attention spans (along with the supporting evidence for the claim)
3. The unrealistic view-of-life claim (including influence and evidence)
4. Gaming applications' effects on a child's school performance
5. Research pertaining to Smart Phones, iPods, and iPads will also be included

Whew! Example 3's paper has the potential to be quite the research project.

Check it out. Do you see how this thesis statement clearly (and powerfully) shows *every single section* of the upcoming paper—and even displays with open arms how the information will be laid out?

BAM. Boom. *Ka-cha!* When you include the three special-sauce ingredients to a thesis statement, explosions, and Kung-fu kicks (not to forget impressive, astonishing, Batman-like *POW!* speech bubbles) are everywhere.

You can do the same—and make your thesis statement just as powerful. No doubt.

Perhaps a good thesis statement is much more than you first thought. Go beyond what you learned in lower-level courses. The thesis statement is so much bigger and better than you can imagine—especially when you use the time-bound element, geographically-bound element, qualification, and blueprinting.

Chapter 39

The Well-Crafted Intro
a.k.a. Your Paper's Shapely Start

All **writing needs some way to begin.** In academic writing, as in most forms of writing, we don't simply begin with the nucleus of our work. That would be like walking into a party and, without saying hello, begin discussing deep physics principles with the first person that we bump into.

We need to introduce ourselves.

The same goes for our paper: Our introductory paragraph is a polite, how-do-you-do moment, drawing interest and putting the reader at ease.

Introductions are oh-so-so important. When you pick up a book for the first time, trying to decide whether or not to read it, what do you do? You
1. look at the title and cover,
2. read the back of the book, and
3. open the book and read the first lines of the first chapter …right?

And if the first paragraph is too boring, too wordy, too dry, not stimulating, hard to follow, or makes you feel like you're lost in a swamp…then forget it. We put the book back on the shelf.

The first lines of your paper are the same (except the instructor can't put your book—er, I mean, your paper—back on the shelf).

First words capture or repel. They pull your eyes in or let your mind wander off into the woods. They get you excited, ready to plunge in with gusto…or make you want to toss the pages and run.

In academia, the first words of your first paragraph set the tone for all of what the instructor thinks of the paper to come. So we have to get the introduction right.

No pressure.

As I've said throughout this entire book, *don't worry*. We've got this covered.

EB Conroy, MA, MFA

Good introductions have a format. That makes writing your first paragraph *much* easier.

The introduction's framework is structured from broad to specific. You need to start like a floodlight and end with laser-beam focus.

It's true. The first line can be amazingly far away from the topic (again, see the next chapter)—yet the last line of the intro has to be spot-on, dead center, on-the-target specific. Whoa. We're talkin' a huge change, from start to finish—in a few, short lines.

How do we do it?

Very, very carefully. Yes, I used the word *very—twice!* (Gasp) Did I get your attention? Good. Fire up your imagination, to start seeing the intro in a 3-D picture.

Think of the first paragraph as a funnel. A physical funnel, one you can hold in your hand. The kind that you use to pour oil into your car engine.

Look at the top of the funnel. It's wide, to capture the splashes. Your reader is as flighty as a splash, by the way. He or she needs to be captured.

The first line of your introduction paragraph has to be as wide as the top diameter of the funnel—ready to catch the reader's attention. The first sentence is not specific. It can be far away from your topic…but it has to be slightly related. Because the first sentence is going to lead your reader to a narrower sentence…and then lead to yet another, more specific sentence…and to a third, more narrow sentence. Each sentence will relate more closely to your topic, until it slides right into the thesis statement, at the bottom of the funnel.

Let's look at the bottom of the funnel. It's narrow, to gather the oil and send it straight down into the engine through a small opening.

The last line (leading into the body of the paper) is the totally-focused, narrow thesis statement—a dynamic sentence crafted to pour the most intense ideas of your upcoming paper into your weighty topic.

And, as we said, just like the funnel, the intro paragraph carries huge movement. Every sentence in-between the broad-rim first sentence and the tight-and-specific thesis statement funnels down, from broad to specific, quite quickly.

Here's an illustration for you: Introductions make me think of hands-on museums that have the giant swirly-doo funnels where you drop a penny in, and it rolls slowly around the entire top edge, gains momentum, and eventually rings itself down into the center. It's a perfect picture of what your introduction should do (but faster).

The parts of an introduction are simple. Within the introductory paragraph, you'll begin with the *hook*. Then you'll use *transition sentenc*es to move the reader to the key point (thesis). Then, ninety-nine percent of the time, you'll end the opening paragraph with the official *thesis statement*. Yes, a thesis statement can move around. But the safe, solid place for the thesis statement in academic writing is the last sentence of the first paragraph. Don't go wandering; keep it there and be safe.

How long is an introduction? A typical introduction is 150 to 200 words. We'll talk about the super-cool starting technique called the *hook* in the next chapter. I simply want to take the time here to talk together about the format of the introduction, so that you have a framework to drop ideas into.

For great introductions, *linear* is the keyword of the day. If you write it right, the linear writing is seamless and fast.

Here are a few examples of linear first paragraphs (used with permission from actual first-year college student papers):

Example 1:

     In a landmark court case on July 21, 1992, Dr. Jack Kevorkian, also known as Dr. Death, was acquitted of the crime of practicing physician-assisted suicide (PAS) after ending the lives of three chronically ill women. That same year, the *Chicago Tribune* stated, "It is time for other doctors to join him and make physician-assisted suicide safe, effective and widely available."[12] Over the past twenty years, PAS has become legal in Montana,[13] Oregon,[14] and Washington.[15] Although advocates of Death with Dignity, a group

---

    [12] Chicago Tribune Wires, "Kevorkian Cleared of Murder Charge," Chicago Tribune, 22 Jul. 1992, sec. 1, p. 3.

    [13] Kirk Johnson, "Montana Ruling Bolsters Doctor Assisted Suicide," New York Times, 31 Dec. 2009 sec. A17.

    [14] Department of Human Services, Oregon Death with Dignity Act Records & Reports, 27 October 1997, available from http://www.oregon.gov/DHS/ph/pas/; Internet; accessed 2 October 2010.

    [15] Washington State Department of Health, Death with Dignity Act, 4 March 2010,

advocating for medically induced death, argue that PAS is an essential, compassionate medical treatment,[16] a closer examination of the practice reveals that PAS is unnecessary, unsafe, and unethical.

The above paragraph is powerfully constructed. There are so many amazing pieces of the puzzle in place, for a powerful opening. Notice that the opening line is chock-full of statistics: July 21, 1992, Kevorkian's name, and a verdict. I'm not always a fan of statistics in the first paragraph, because it's hard to do well, but when you can make stats work, more power to you.

The paragraph's opening line leads us down the funnel to more specific information—supported by footnotes giving the paper an immediate sense of academic strength.

Notice, too, the writer's strong and emotionally powerful words: *acquitted, crime, suicide, chronically ill, death, unnecessary, unsafe,* and *unethical.* Now notice what I call *diamond words*—words that powerfully draw the reader in: *landmark, dignity, advocating, essential, compassionate,* and *examination.* This writer knows how to grab specific nouns and dynamic action verbs. The word choice is also known as *syntax.* When your syntax is right-on, your ideas tend to be stronger.

Finally, note how each line flows into the other with a little more intensity, right up to the thesis at the end. And all of that was accomplished in 187 words. Nice job, Kira.

Example 2:
    Imagine a perfect world where every person has a job, a house, a nice salary, and health insurance. Some say the prosperous world exists for all, with the use of a marvelous tool: Keynesian stimulus. Accordingly, if governments spend a vast amount of money when economic trouble occurs, the economy will tend to recover and people will prosper.[17] However, the perfect world will never be. Although some economists and political leaders contend that the government should spend money during a recession to cause the economy to rebound, Keynesian stimulus in a modern, capitalistic economy during a recession or depression actually stifles immediate growth

---

available from http://www.doh.wa.gov/dwda/; Internet; accessed 3 October 2010.

[16] Technically, the student should have a footnote for this portion.

[17] Brian Snowdown and Howard R. Vane, *Modern Macroeconomics: Its Origins, Development and Current State* (Northampton: Edward Elgar Publishing Limited, 2005) 410.

and damages economic prospects for years.

Can you find all of the fabulous, good-introduction secret weapons hiding in the paragraph above? The opening line is broad, pleasant, and conversational in style (and uses the word, *imagine,* which is a declaration with proven emotional pull in all forms of writing). At first blush, the opening line doesn't seem to connect at all with words like *Keynesian* and *economy.* That's what makes it such a nice *hook.*

Just like a fishing hook disguised by a rubber worm, the paragraph's first line seems innocuous and lures the reader in.

The second line draws us quickly into the topic of the paper—an amazing zeroing in on academic thought (who woulda thunk your imagination floating around in the perfect world would plop you into economics!).

Equally as fast, you're sped along the highway to a footnoted idea that slams on the breaks with a short-and-powerful statement: "However, the perfect world will never be." Ooh. We agree with the statement, don't we? And now, we're really wondering where this writer is going.

And then, *ta-da!* You're standing face to face with the bright laser light of a strong, complete thesis statement. Check out the *diamond words* along the way: *perfect, prosperous, exists, marvelous tool, vast, trouble, prosper, leaders content, modern, capitalistic economy, recession, depression, stifles immediate growth, damages economic prospects*—whoa! All powerful! The resulting first paragraph is a pleasure to read. Bravo, Christopher!

Example 3:

Nearly one-fifth of the world's population resides in China. With a gross domestic product of $4.222 trillion, a workforce comprised of approximately 808 million people, and an economic growth rate of 9.8 percent, China has emerged quickly on the world stage.[18] According to the Council on Foreign Relations, the US-China relationship is the most crucial foreign policy issue in the 21st century.[19] Over the last 30 years, US presidents

---

[18] "Background Note: China," US Department of State, http://www.state.gov/r/pa/ei/bgn/18902.htm (accessed December 5, 2009).

[19] Ashton Carter, Carla Hills, Dennis Blair, Frank Sampson Jannuzi et al. *US-China Relations: An Affirmative Agenda, A Responsible Course* (New York: Report for Council on Foreign Relations Press, 2007), 11, http://www.cfr.org/publication/12985/ (accessed December 5, 2009).

have taken different approaches to America's crucial relationship with China. The recent transition of power from the Bush administration to the Obama administration is no exception. Although President Obama has emulated some aspects of the Bush administration's policies toward China, the president has already taken definitive steps to change US-China policies in two key areas: the economy and human rights.

The previous paragraph leans heavily on academic content and style, for success. The opening is a *startling statistic* hook, followed by another startling statistic, followed by another startling statistic. Hat trick!

And there's more. When the writer states, "China has emerged quickly on the world stage," you have no problem believing the claim.

The statement about the transition of administrations is also a transition to the purpose and main idea of the paper (brilliant!). And the thesis stands strong. Diamond words abound. Punctuation (the colon) supports the strong throw-it-forward movement at the end. And the reader is left with no question as to the intent of the paper. Good work, Alicia.

Give your introduction shape. Let the ideas slide smoothly from broad to specific. It takes skill—and time—to make a shapely introduction. Take the time.

One more note: You'll find more writing examples and how-to goodness in other books in the *Simplified Writing* series. I'm giving you a commercial here because you might be saying to yourself, *I wish there were more examples of this that I can learn from.* So, I wanted you to know, you can. That's good news.

Chapter 40

Hook 'em In and Move 'em Out
a.k.a. The First Line Catch

I adore *hooks*. Not fishing hooks. (I tend to get bored with fishing. But that's just me.) I adore using hooks in writing. Whether it's a fiction story or a graduate-level paper at a university, get a great hook, write a great intro, and you start with a good impression—and the reader sticks with you, straight to the end.

There are four major ways to hook your reader, so that he or she gets interested in what you have to say and stays with you. This page covers the four major types, along with specific how-to details. To make this an easy reference page, I've put everything into a handy-dandy format. Enjoy.

Hook 1: Knock their socks off
A. Use **startling statistics**—numbers that jump off the page with meaning.
B. Use a **startling quote**—a fact or prediction making your reader sit up and get excited...or, at least, startled (hence the name).

The knock their socks off mantra is, *shake up the reader, keep the reader.* Of course, the shaking is a good kind of shaking, with no pain involved...just a surprise, like saying, *boo.*

Hook 2: Grab their emotions
A. Pull in emotions with **scare tactics**: numbers, quotes, or general info that's scary and makes the reader say, *whooooaaaa...say it isn't so!*
B. Make an emotional connection with **warm fuzzies**—info that makes your reader feel good inside and, therefore, want to continue reading.
C. You'll grab emotions when you **paint a picture**—writing a few lines of a tantalizing, unique, or flavorful impression that tickles the reader's appreciation of the senses.
D. Emotions can be stirred with a **quote by an admirable character;** whether Socrates or Ben Franklin, the name grabs the reader with emotion.
E. **Create an emotional bond, as a colleague**: Call out the reader's name. By saying your audience's title, such as teachers, instructors, Republicans, or whomever you're writing to, you make an emotional connection. You and I like to emotionally connect with kindred spirits.

Hook 3: Tell a story (albeit a short one)

A. You can tell a story with **words that are** *benefit-based*—telling the reader what he or she will get, by reading the piece.

B. You can tell **a story that is** *fear-based*—telling the reader something negative, something that he or she knows to avoid, feeding on the reader's morbid curiosity, worries, suspicions, and uncertainties.

C. Your story can be in the form of **colorful, evocative, or eloquent language**: lush words and descriptors that aren't used anywhere else in the paper.

Yes, you can get away with using story in an academic paper…if it's short and effectively used as a hook. Storytelling has captured hearts for thousands of years. Capture your reader right off the bat with your own *once upon a time.*

Hook 4: Make them think

A. The most common way to get your reader thinking is to **ask a question.** Our brains are wired to find answers to questions. Get the reader answering a question in his or her mind, and he or she is hooked.

B. An intriguing way to invoke a response is to **propose a** *what if?* **question**—again, to get the reader engaged and involved in your topic right away.

C. Finally, **ask a** *do you, can you, will you, should you,* **or** *could you* **question**—and, again, you'll make the reader's connection to your writing right away.

Questions make the line taught, ready to pull the reader into the rest of the intro…into your thesis…and into your paper, right up to the conclusion.

How long is a hook? The trick is, your hook needs to be short—one to three sentences. At times, with longer papers, you can get away with a whole paragraph (as in the *tell a story* hook)…but most of the time, your hook will be one sentence.

There are so many great ways to hook your reader in. When drafting your work, don't simply craft one hook; try making two or three. Then ask someone near and dear to you which hook reads the best. Hooks are one of the most fun parts of your paper. Take the time to craft a sharp hook, to whet your reader's appetite for more.

Chapter 41

Slide in Source Info
a.k.a. Quote, Summarize, and Paraphrase

A source is any place you find information that you're going to insert inside your written work. Amazing information can come from a book, a newspaper, a magazine, and online article, a web site, a conversation (interview), and even a DVD cover—each one is a *source*. I cover sources in depth in the *Simplified Research Writing* book—where to get good source materials, the best ones to get, and so on. But for now, we'll simply pretend we already have our quotes and facts in the palms of our hands. Let's chat about how to properly insert the information inside our PEAsy paragraphs.

There are three quite-easy-PEAsy ways to incorporate source material into our essays and papers:
1. Direct quote
2. Summary
3. Paraphrase

Direct quotes have a usual resting place in the paragraph: Traditionally, we place quotes in the middle of the paragraph. Note, I said *traditionally,* which means that there will be plenty of times when the direct quote won't follow what I'm telling you here. So why am I even bothering?

Here's why: I'd love for you to use the instruction here as a baseline, to start sliding in quotations of support. Once comfortable with using quotes to support ideas, you can be more liberal with the source information's position in the paragraph.

Here's how a center-of-the-paragraph quotation works:

Sentence one is the tantalizing topic sentence. It tells the reader your position on the topic. It's your key point. The first sentence is the claim or the assertion. We already know all about topic sentences, don't we? Yeppers. So I know you get it.

Sentence two sets up the quote. It's a clarification, elucidation, amplification, or illumination sentence that tells us a tiny bit more about the first sentence. It gives perhaps a detail or two more, so that we know where the author is going with the point.

The third sentence is where we slide in the quote. The quote "proves" to the reader that your topic sentence wasn't just blowing smoke. Your quote comes from a super-fancy expert's words on the topic—showing that you didn't just abracadabra the idea out of the air. Other people—*important* people—happen to say what you said, too. The quote, sitting in the third sentence spot, comes just in time—just when your reader is saying to himself, "Oh yeah? Who says so?" And then you show us who says so.

Sentence four can either be a sentence explaining the quote a bit, or you can put in a second quote. If the first quote was strong and impressive, we may not need another quote. We'll simply write a next sentence that expounds on the impressive quote, because the impressive quote worked quite nicely, thank you. But if you have a second quote (particularly from a different source) that says the same thing as the first, using the second quote can bolster your point. If *two* experts say the same thing, back-to-back, our reader will most likely be awed. Awed readers are good. That mean's we're coming across well.

At this point, we have four sentences. Most paragraphs do the job well with between five and seven sentences.

So sentence five can be the conclusion of the paragraph—the wrap up statements summarizing the gist of the entire thing.

Or you can drop in more—repeating sentence types three and four again (another quote and its explanation). Then wrap up the paragraph

Either way, you've followed the formula. And *ta-da*. We're ready for the next paragraph. That's how you shape your academic paragraph.

Before you go on to the next paragraph, make sure the details of quotations are correct. Double quotation marks have to sit around the exact words…not single. Always, always, always—frame the text coming *directly* from the source inside the quotes. If you want to give the general idea from the source, you can do that. Place your citation footnote right after the borrowed material.

Remember, the footnote comes directly after the quote, as so:

"Here is my quote."[20]

Another detail: If the quote is *inside* the sentence, "as in the portion right here,"[21] the order of elements is quote, comma, end quotation mark, footnote, space, and move on. That's exactly what I did, in the *as in the portion right here* part, above. There. Those are the details.

Let's move on to the second way to place a quote within the paper. It's called the *block quotation,* or *offset quote.*

The block quote, or offset quote, comes by its name naturally: Its rectangular shape on the page looks like a brick or cinder block. And the block is off-set (set off) from the left margin. Here's what an offset quote looks like in Turabian/Chicago Style:

> The words that you're reading right now are in a block, or offset, quote format. Unlike the single-spaced lines of the book in your hands, the text of your college-level paper is double spaced....Until you have a long piece of text to quote (like this). Long pieces of quoted material are treated like princes and princesses, with special-privilege format. You see, for a block quotation, the lines are single-spaced. Also, the left side of the block quote is flush left at the indent (or tab) area...making the block visually set off from the rest of the text. Notice: The block doesn't have an indent. And there are no quotation marks at the start or at the end of the block. In Turabian Style, you have to have at least five lines of text. You probably don't want to have a block quotation any longer than what you see here. If you have this much info, please think about summarizing or paraphrasing. Thanks.[22]

Finally, double space before and after the off-set text. Between the text and block quote (both the before and afterward portions of white space), Microsoft Word programs tend to automatically give you more space than double. So be the detail-oriented editor. Check your block quote's before-and-after spacing, before turning in your paper.

For those of you who have to learn parenthetical citations...here's an example that isn't a footnote: "Blah, blah, blah and some more blah"

---

[20] Here's where my footnote goes, for the end-of-the-sentence quote.

[21] Here's where my footnote goes, for the in-the-middle-of-the-sentence quote.

[22] And this is where the footnote goes, for the block (or offset) quotation.

(Conroy, 2014). Then, on the References page, you'll find an entry for me, under that year, with the rest of the citation information lined up. More on that in the other book, *Simplified Research Writing*. (Check it out.)

Chapter 42

Make Your Reader Walk Away with Point in Hand
a.k.a. Make the "So What?" Pop from Your Conclusion

So what? That's the question that your reader constantly asks. Yep. At the end of whatever you wrote, "So what?" echoes in your reader's head.

In other words...
"What's the point?"
"What's the big deal?"
"So why did I read this, anyway?"

So what is also the question your professor has walking around in his or her brain. If you want a good grade, then you'd better find your *so what* a seat.

In other words, your teacher or professor is asking...
"What's the bottom line?"
"Did this student show me what he or she knows?"
"Am I walking away with a key idea that makes sense?"

And let's hear it for the most famous thought of all ...
"Am I challenged to think differently or to do anything differently, because I read this piece?"

If your reader can't walk away knowing the key point, you've failed.
Ooh. That's harsh. But it's also reality. So, instead of sitting here, let's roll up our sleeves and take a look at the final idea together.

In academic writing, everything should be squeezed into a final idea.
The final idea is the one—not two, not three, not thirty ideas, but the *one* idea—that is key. Foundational. Critical. As in, *I want my reader to walk away with this truth*. Period.

Yes, your essay, your paper, your thesis, or your dissertation may have many ideas presented. But in order to be a successful communicator, you'll need to have one prominent, preeminent truth.

That walk-away truth can be an idea or an action. In a comparison and contrast essay for a literature course, the truth might be, "Authors C.S. Lewis

EB Conroy, MA, MFA

and Isaac Asimov, though both speculative fiction writers, exhibit distinct differences in content and style." In a government class's argumentative paper, the truth for the writer will be the assertion or claim: "Overall, capitalism is more profitable for both the individual and the country." In a final exam essay for a psychology class, the truth might be, "If families integrate Daniel Goleman's ideas of Emotional Intelligence (EI) into their high school students' daily lives, students will earn higher grades in college." The *so what* one-liner bursts with flavor.

More times than not, the *so what* statement resides in your written work's final paragraph. That final paragraph, as most of you know, is called the conclusion. What do you do in the conclusion? Duh, you say: You conclude. End. Close. Finish. Wrap it up and say goodbye. But let's say goodbye on good terms, shall we?

To say goodbye to your reader on good terms, you must be sure that your conclusion is complete. When we miss something in the conclusion, the reader is left hanging, feeling empty and sad. Sometimes the reader feels gypped…then angry. Let's not go there, eh? Let's make the conclusion strong.

Yes, the conclusion is a shapely paragraph. Here's how:

1. You will revisit main points. Notice that I didn't say *parrot back* the main points. You'll need to give the points with a twist, a new essence, that's not a verbatim list.

2. Your conclusion will use summary. Make bullet-pointish claims that pull your sections' ideas together. No, you won't really put in bullet points. You will hammer off the most powerful ideas in a lucid, smooth-move way.

3. Your conclusion will move the reader along linearly. As you write your sentences linearly, each successive sentence will move you closer to the truth statement—the *so what* at the end.

4. Your conclusion will go global. Oh, yes—we can't forget—at the very end, where you leave the reader totally awed by your amazing prowess at pulling together your powerful ideas, you'll want to make the ideas go global: Be big, broad, and brassy. Think *how does this affect my reader's world?*

5. You may even use cool techniques in your last sentence—techniques that you're familiar with, with the hook. Echo what worked at the beginning of your paper. Use a question. Or bookend with a quote that's similar, parallel to, or a continuation of the quote used in your opening. You may even tell the end of the story that you began in the introduction.

The conclusion gets to use all of these amazing, shapely ideas and more. I love the fact that the first and last lines of an academic work can be rule-breakers.

Always end with your work with a sense of the bottom line. Don't let the reader have to guess what your writing was all about. Be specific, clear, and strong. In many ways, the last paragraph isn't *so what*. It's *that's what. There it is. Take it and do something with it.*

SECTION 8

Write and Revise in Style:
Sweep 'em Off Their Feet

Chapter 43

Be Stylish to a T
a.k.a. Dress for Your Audience

I'm hoping that, by now, you're *feeling the mood* of the academic style of writing. It's a special mood, with special style. Academic writing is not like hip hop. It's not like jazz. It's not even like ballet. It's certainly not the mood of Broadway or Bollywood dancing (for those of you who don't know about Bollywood, look it up … it could make you smile). No, academic writing is more like ballroom dancing. We have to wear tuxes and formal dresses. That's the style.

What is *style*? Style refers to the *way* that you write, as opposed to *what* you write. Style is the words you choose, the way that you arrange the sentences and paragraphs, and your tone—all wrap together into the Christmas present of *style*.

In academic writing, your job is to purposefully create a style. Nothing is haphazard. It's all planned. Every centimeter of your work is crafted to specific parameters.

Your audience expects perfection:
* An introduction with a hook, narrowing sentences, and a thesis statement that clearly blueprints your paper's intent
* A thesis statement with a qualification, premise, time-bound element, and geographically-bound element
* Well-chosen words that are high-level, placed in sentences that vary in length and have a rhythm
* Sentences that are clear, concise, and well-articulated
* Paragraphs using only one topic, with parallelism, transitions, and connectives for cohesiveness—formed with a claim, examples and support, and finished with a wrap up or transition forward
* Information placed in a logical order, answering the reader's questions before they're asked, so that all is linear and smooth
* A conclusion answering the *so what*

That's all.

Actually, think of your writing as origami. Each of the single bits of information that you've learned in this book is like a single fold, in origami. If you make each fold correctly, then in the end, the origami form will turn out beautifully. With style.

Chapter 44

There are Many Ways to Write Well
a.k.a. Good, Better, and Different Better

We all know by now that, in academic writing, the way that you arrange your words really matters. But the cool thing is this: There are many right ways to arrange words. Writing has flexibility, and that flexibility includes artistic flair. You get to pick what works best for you, in your own personal style, as you write. Writing is artsy. And art can vary.

However, there *is* such a thing as bad writing and good writing. You have to meet the guidelines of good writing first, in order to be able to be flexible in your artistic style and flair. It's kind of like jazz musicians having to learn scales and arpeggios before improvising. So let's talk about the scales and arpeggios of good writing.

First, good writing communicates ideas. If you aren't communicating clearly, then you can call the writing *bad*. Whatever the message or information that you're trying to get across to your reader, you must communicate it clearly, in order to meet the definition of good writing.

Second, good writing is effortless to absorb. You can follow good writing's line of thinking, from start to finish. It makes sense to you, and it's easy to take in. If you have to work at understanding and absorbing the writing, then the writing can be considered *bad*. The reader must read and absorb the information seamlessly and easily, for your work to be considered good writing.

Third, good writing meets its purpose. Remember, all writing is for a reason. If your reason for writing your paper was to persuade, but the reader wasn't swayed in the least, then the paper wasn't good writing. If your reason was to inform, but when the reader finished your work, it felt like something was left out, then your writing wasn't good. The reader has to leave with a sense of satisfaction that your paper's purpose was met.

Fourth, good writing is technically correct. Punctuation, grammar, and capitalization count. Your ideas can be stellar, but if you can't place a comma to save your life, then your writing is not good writing. And it goes both ways. You can have a technically clean paper, but if the content isn't meeting the purpose, easy to absorb, and full of ideas that are communicated clearly, then your writing isn't good.

Okay, let's say that you have the basics of good writing in place. Now what? Now you get to play with it. There are many right ways to write an idea. Any number of ways can be considered good, and don't let anyone tell you differently. There are a whole lot of people walking around, thinking that their way is the best way. And there are many variations of good.

However…if you're writing anything other than expressive writing (a personal journal or poem, created only for you) and your reader doesn't like what you've wrote—then you have a big problem on your hands. You're supposed to be writing for the reader. You have to satisfy the reader.

It's a delicate balance, isn't it? You have to find the *right way to connect with the reader.* So keep in mind that the reader is your customer. Our job is to make customers happy.

Chapter 45

Answer the Reader's Question before the Reader Breathes
a.k.a. "What Will They Think of Next?"

The absolute best writers answer the readers' questions—even before that little thought bubble appears above the reader's head.

Let's play a game.
If I write *blue*, what do ninety percent of all readers ask?
What is blue?

And if I write *blue ocean*, what do ninety percent of all readers ask?
Which ocean?

And if I write *blue Pacific Ocean*, what do ninety percent of all readers ask?
What about the Pacific Ocean?

Do you see how it works? Conjure up an idea of what you believe that ninety percent of readers will ask, then write that information next. If you answer the reader's question before the reader breathes, then the readers' minds travel along a smooth track at a good clip-clop, with the wind in their hair and smiles on their faces. With that kind of smooth ride, most readers are happy.

Let's do it again.
I write, *I believe this is going to be a great weekend.*
What do you ask? *Why? What's going on this weekend?*

I write, *we're going to watch a movie.*
What do you ask? *What movie are you going to see?*

I write, *we're watching Les Miserables.*
What do you say? *Oh—cool. Who stars in the movie?*

I write, *the film features many of my favorite actors, including Hugh Jackman, Russell Crowe, and Anne Hathaway.*

Now check this out: Here's what the above information looks like, when I take out the questions:

I believe this is going to be a great weekend because we're going to watch the movie, Les Miserables. The film features many of my favorite actors, including Hugh Jackman, Russell Crowe, and Anne Hathaway.

That's smooth. Seamless. Satisfying to the mind. Let's do one more—this time, with an academic topic.
I write, *childhood obesity can have a harmful effect on the body in a variety of ways.*
The reader asks, *in what ways does obesity harm a child's body?*

I write, *first, obese children are more likely to have high blood pressure.*
The reader asks, *what does high blood pressure to do a child?*

I write, *high blood pressure often causes no noticeable discomfort; but headache, dizziness, shortness of breath, visual disturbances, and fatigue may indicate high blood pressure in a child.*

The reader asks, *how else is obesity harmful to children?*
I write, *childhood obesity can also cause breathing problems such as sleep apnea.*

The reader asks, *what is sleep apnea?*
I write, *sleep apnea is a sleep disorder set apart by atypical pauses in breathing or abnormally low breathing, during sleep.*

Here's our information from above, minus the questions:
Childhood obesity can have a harmful effect on the body in a variety of ways. First, obese children are more likely to have high blood pressure. High blood pressure often causes no noticeable discomfort, but headache, dizziness, shortness of breath, visual disturbances, and fatigue may indicate high blood pressure in a child. Childhood obesity can also cause breathing problems such as sleep apnea, which is a sleep disorder set apart by atypical pauses in breathing or abnormally low breathing, during sleep.

You have to admit, that's pretty cool. And I can write a whole paper this way, can't I?

Or maybe you could.

SECTION 9

Creating the Final Product

Chapter 46

Do it Now
a.k.a. Procrastination is a Dirty Word

"Hi, my name is Erin…and I'm a procrastinator."** Are you in the club, too?

Someone once told me that writers come in two flavors: *Writer-Thinkers* and *Thinker-Writers*. Let me explain.

A *Writer-Thinker* is a person who writes out his or her ideas—exactly as the ideas come into consciousness. The stream-of-consciousness writer gets a bit crazy with the words, because everything flies out onto the paper at once. Thoughts splat and flitter and meander all over the place. The Writer-Thinker is also called the *Writer Drafter*—because he or she drafts in a kind of throw-it-onto-the-paper way…and has to clean up the mess afterward with mega editing sessions.

A *Thinker-Writer* is a person who thinks about the writing, first. And thinks…and thinks…and thinks…until the Thinker-Writer throws out all of the ideas at once, in one giant rush—like a fire hose blasting onto the paper. The amazing thing is, what comes out of the Thinker-Writer is actually pretty ordered and sometimes pretty-near complete. Why? Because drafting already happened inside of the Thinker-Writer's head.

The Thinker-Writer propensity is a blessing and a curse. The blessing is that, for a Thinker-Writer, writing can be a super-fun rush (it's downright exciting to hold the fire hose and feel the surge of creativity blast onto the page). The curse (you can hear it coming) is that Thinker-Writers may spend time too much time thinking.

Enter the scene: Procrastination.

Procrastination is defined as *waiting too long to get your behind into gear.* It's not having enough time to get the job done. It's pressure. Stress. Anxiety. Totally uncomfortable. And definitely not anywhere near the definition of *pleasant.*

Procrastinate, and you lose. You lose sleep (pulling those all-nighters), energy (because you lost sleep), and grades (because you were half asleep when you wrote the words on the paper). Eventually, you lose self-respect. Possibly, you lose a future job. Finally, you lose enjoyment of the writing process—and your ability to live up to your potential.

How do we solve the problem of procrastination? Well, that answer is as individual as each of us. But here are five simple suggestions that might help keep your fingers sticking to the keys and clicking along like they're supposed to be doing.

1. Make a schedule...and keep it. Make a date with yourself. Make it a quiet place where you can focus. Then keep the date.

2. Break the task down into simple pieces. Don't look at the whole thing. Work on one piece at one time.

3. Show your progress. Cross off a calendar square...make a list...use a row of check boxes...anything to show that you're moving forward. Forward movement acts like the proverbial snowball, getting bigger and stronger with momentum. Start packing the snow now.

4. Be accountable. Get someone on your back, keeping track of your progress and giving you a pep talk, when needed. We all work better when someone's watching our back.

5. Give yourself rewards. When you finish a piece, do something small but fun. When you finish the entire assignment, throw yourself a party...*anything* to celebrate.

Beware: Procrastination stalks more than just Thinker-Writers. The beast can swallow up anybody. Do you remember the Writer-Thinkers— those chaps sitting with the messy draft that came out onto the page right away? Well, the Writer-Thinkers usually get bogged down, too—when needing to clean up their project's draft. The daunting thought of editing the mess is enough to drive anyone to procrastination.

If you're a Writer-Thinker, be conscious of your tendency to freeze up in the editing process. Then refer to the list of five procrastination-breakers above.

Yes, I'm a Thinker-Writer...and I tend to procrastinate. How about you? Are you like me, or are you a Writer-Thinker? Either way, it's worth fighting the pull to procrastinate. Because the bottom line is this: Procrastination makes for poor writing results. Conquer procrastination, and you'll not only feel better—but you'll also (most likely) get a better grade.

Chapter 47

Do it Again…and Again…and Again…
a.k.a. Writers Write Until it's Right

I don't know one person on the face of this earth who can write anything worth anything in a first sitting. Seriously…the Declaration of Independence had *how* many drafts?! (Some sources say up to 80.) A famous Young Adult fiction writer that I know says that her latest bestseller had 27 drafts and three complete endings. Author Stephen King, in his book *On Writing*, shows readers some of his editor's thick black slashes and requests for clarity on his eventual bestsellers.

Do it again isn't the exception; it's the norm.

I'm convinced: Good writing occurs only within the repetition of rewrites. With that said, it's only normal, then, to *expect* to write over and over and over. Any other expectation is false.

So it's time to change your expectations. Don't expect to sit at the keyboard and pop out a masterpiece in one sitting (or even two). It won't happen. Instead, expect to make time to write a draft, have someone look at it, then to write again. And to go over it again. And to go over it again.

Get this: Repetition is not your enemy. Writing, rewriting, and writing again are the welcoming party to a grand hoopla event called *excellence*.

Your best friend is the person who tells you what's wrong. In order to rewrite well, you'll need quality feedback.

Notice I said *quality* feedback. You need a good editing guide—someone who can give you quality comments. As with traveling over any wild terrain, those who have gone before are the best guides. Your mom is bound to say, "Oooh, I love it!" Your classmate is bound to say, "Yeah, that's great"…when you work isn't great at all. Never ask a classmate for help, either. They're simply not qualified to give you the best advice.

Finding an impartial editor who knows what they're talking about is important to your success. So when I refer to *your editor*, I'm referring to someone who knows what he or she is doing (like an instructor, published writer, or friend who has been trained well in the art of editing).

Yes, editors are fabulous friends. What's more important is that you accept their friendship (in the form of honest feedback). If your editor-person says that something doesn't make sense, then don't defend yourself and explain why the writing is good. Don't whisper under your breath that they simply don't *get* it. There's nothing to get. If your editor-friend says something's wrong, then most likely, something's wrong. Instead of defending yourself, listen. For the reader's opinion is paramount. Take the comments with grace. Then change what you wrote.

Here are a few helpful hints, for how to check and rewrite academic papers (in order of completion):

1. Check that your draft follows your outline's main points. One quick way to check for outline-matching is to read the first sentences (the topic sentences) of all of your paragraphs, in a row, aloud. Your first sentences should make total sense together, as you read through the paper.

2. Check the size of your paper's sections. Each section should be relatively similar in size—or, at the least, should match the outline's section size. If a section is unreasonably fatter than the rest and needs to go on a diet, then by all means, slim down by taking away calories (extra words and sentences).

3. See if a section, paragraph, or sentence needs to be moved. Most times, content must be rearranged. Your writing might be out of order. *Expect* your writing to be out of order. Look for it. Rearrange sections and lines to make your writing flow.

4. Check that each paragraph is unto itself. Is that thought, phrase, or sentence extra, not completely fitting under the paragraph's main idea? If so, then throw it out.

5. Save editing details for last. When you start the rewrite process, don't get caught in choosing that special word or fixing all of the commas. Keep yourself from laser beam hyper focus. Think floodlight. Then flashlight. Then laser.

Don't let yourself believe the lie that rewriting and editing is for sissies. Rewriting is normal and expected. Write until it's right.

Chapter 48

Use Editors' Eyes
a.k.a. Don't Trust Your Vision

Let's continue our revising and editing momentum. Editors are our friends. Editors bring good news. Editors help us. If you don't have an editor, it's time to go out and get one.

The reason that we need an editor is to save us from ourselves. And there are two reasons why we need to save us from ourselves. (Yes, in writing, we can be our own worst enemy.)

Frankly, we're too close to the product, to see our writing's flaws. We've read our creation over and over, and we've become too familiar with it. Everything looks good, to our eyes. We need an editor to point to the page and say, "That's not working."

Second, we are too close to our writing emotionally, to see the flaws and to kick them out the door. We loooooove what we wrote. We want to huuuuuug and hoooooold our words, phrases, sentences, and paragraphs (and perty-darn-near the entire thing that we wrote)—because we've developed a warm-and-fuzzy affinity for our words. Just as we have a hard time saying no to a friend, we have a hard time saying no to tossing out part of our writing—even if it's causing all kinds of problems.

Good editors help us to see the flaws, and good editors are honest— telling us what needs fixing and what needs to be vaporized.

But what if you don't have—and can't find—an editor? I'll take issue with that assumption. I believe that anyone can find an editor…someone who has some writing experience and know-how. We may be hard to find, but we're out here. Family members may have skills (although, as stated earlier, there may be problems with family). Some college students will gladly give editing feedback. Neighbors, business associates, former educators…they're all out there, and I'm sure that someone is willing to help.

For special writing, such as an essay for a scholarship, you may have to ramp up the editing quality. With a super important piece of writing in the oven, you want the words cooked up right—and if you have the funds to make it happen, then you may want to hire someone to do the job right.

Finally, if you're taking a class or course, contact your instructor for help. I'm always surprised by the number of students who don't contact me until the end of the semester and then say, "Oh, man, I should have contacted you earlier!" Uh…yes. I'm more than happy to help. Most instructors are.

Okay—so let's say that you really are stuck, and you haven't found your editor yet. Then, at the least, read your writing out loud. Whisper it. Speak it. Even record it.

Something magical happens when we read our work aloud. The errors pop out. The rhythm exposes itself. Fragments and run on sentences squirm in discomfort, because they know they've been found. Reading aloud is our back-pocket last-chance effort, to get some shade of editing into our masterpiece. Use it. Every time.

And then go searching for that editor-person.

Chapter 49

A Word on Submissions and Communicating with Professors
a.k.a. The Right and Wrong Way to Write an Email

Today, electronic communication is a way of life. Days are filled with texting, messaging, posting on Twitter and Facebook, and IMing. With the exorbitant amount of informal writing bouncing off of the satellites that circle our planet, it was only a matter of time that a sense of chummy, relaxed conversation would elbow its way into our academic writing world.

Brace yourself: Because if you want to succeed in formal academics, then it's time to sit up straight and get back to formal writing in Academia Land.

When communicating with your professors (or anybody else on our Big Blue World), you project an image. Your image sets a tone—and develops a persona, communication style, and relationship with your professor that sends positive or negative vibes.

What kind of vibes do you want to send to your professors? If you want life to go well in Academia Land, your goal should be to make the best professional connection. You want your instructor to recognize your skills, share respect, and yes, think highly of you.

So let's get down to business. Here's a list of 20 do's and don'ts for email communication with your professors:

1. Start with a professional greeting. You know what I mean: Something like, "Dear Professor So-and-so" qualifies. But "Hey," "Hi there," and "Yo" don't cut it. Also, leaving out a greeting (starting right into the text) is improper. Give your instructor respect from the get-go. Start with a proper greeting.

2. Don't talk in text language. lol (laugh out loud), jw (just wondering), and lower-case "i" for referring to yourself ("I") are all examples of text-talk that you shouldn't ever use within an email to your professor. It's unprofessional.

3. Don't use buddy-buddy phrases. Honestly, don't tell your instructor, "Just kidding" or "you know what I mean." Your instructor is not your roommate. You have a professor-student relationship that's closer to a Star Wars Jedi-Padawan relationship than pals who live across the street from each other. When it comes to an instructor, be kind and friendly, but keep professional boundaries intact.

4. Capitalize properly. Yes, the Shift key still works for emails. Use it. And with contractions (like "don't"), the apostrophe key still works, too.

5. Use paragraph structure. One gigantic block of words and sentences is unsightly—and not unlike the dynamics of an acquaintance at a party talking your ear off for ten minutes. Use topic sentences with a main idea, similar-content sentences, and conclusion statements. Make your writing shapely, with form, direction, and purpose….even in an email.

6. Write in complete sentences, with proper grammar. With each word that you type, you're leaving an impression. Grammar usage adds or takes away from that impression. Make the impression a good one.

7. After the greeting, use a "door opener." *Door openers* are connecting phrases that open the reader to personal connection. The phrase, "Thank you for your comments on my paper," is a good opener (if it's true); "I enjoyed this week's discussion board topic" is another good door opener (again, if it's true). Stating a positive and professional phrase at the beginning of your email helps to open the door to your email readers' mind and heart.

8. Show appreciation. Be sincere. "Thank you" and "I appreciate your time" are wonderful ways to show gratitude and make a positive connection with your instructor. But don't butter up; be honest and sensible. Instructors can see through buttery extra calories in your words.

9. Use your Spell Check. It's a great tool that can save you from embarrassment. But don't rely completely on the Spell Check. As a quick self-editing technique, read your email out loud before you send it. Mistakes often show up with a verbal reading.

10. Save the subject line for the subject. Don't put the entire email message in the subject line and leave the email blank. Write the email.

11. Don't forward popular emails to your instructors. If there is an item that's academically related to the course, cut and paste the information into an attached document—or better yet, send an email that asks your professor if they are interested in seeing the material, before sending. Don't waste your instructor's time with forwards that aren't related to the course content.

12. Save emoticons for siblings, parents, grandparents, and friends. Emoticons are fun for friends and family. Don't "share" smiley faces and frowns with your instructors.

13. Make sure you're sending the email to the correct person. As an instructor, it's embarrassing to receive a personal email meant for someone else. And I'm sure that you'll be quite embarrassed to know that I heard about you and your friend's date.

14. If you attach a file to the email, make note of the attachment within the email body. Tell the instructor that Assignment A is attached. And before you send the email, make sure that the attachment is indeed attached.

15. Whether sending an email from a laptop, Smart Phone or iPad, write a complete email. Avoid short cuts. Writing a proper email may take you longer, but it's the appropriate thing to do.

16. Sign your first and last name to the email. Don't assume that your instructor knows you on a first-name basis (or knows whose email they're reading). And unless you have an email signature, always use both names.

17. Signature lines are okay to use, if professional. Titles, business logos, and classy famous quotes are acceptable. Off-color jokes or phrases aren't.

18. Show basic respect in the words you choose. With an instructor, you are in a subordinate position. It's a good position—one of learning from and deferring to. Keep the position intact.

A final word: You have a choice as to whether or not you'll follow these guidelines. Give yourself credit. You are capable and intelligent. Leave a positive impression.

EB Conroy, MA, MFA

Chapter 50

Let it Go and Celebrate!
a.k.a. When it's Finished, Shake Hands, Smile, and Move On

Whenever we create, there is a moment when the creation is finished. A composer writes his final note. An artist decides it's the last brush stroke. A writer finally stops and says, *no more words; the writing is complete.* Or so it seems.

I present to you the idea that, no matter what you write, you'll most likely come back to the piece and say *that needs more work; it's not finished*. Even when it's finished, the work may not feel finished.

It's true. Think about your own life. How many of us have come back one year, one month, one week, or even one 24-hour-period later to say, "Oh, man—I wish I could do that differently. I'd change this…and this…and this…"? Such is the nature of creating art.

And writing is an art form. Art can be presented many, many, many (did I say *many*?) ways and still be considered good art. The new piece is not necessarily better; it's simply changed into a form called *different.*

I always say, there are many ways to write well. Our sentence can be transformed into a beautiful piece by simply changing a word or rearranging the sentence's structure. Yes, one version may be stronger than the other. But what's to say that the first version is not a form of good as well? Yet another version may give the reader a feeling unique from the first two renditions.

Different has to do with the *flavor* of the writing. Flavor is good. So let's embrace the fact that there are many ways to write well, through the dynamic of *difference.*

You can always write it differently. And you will always become a better writer. At some point, though, you must call the work *finished.* So do your best, stop, and let it go. As in saying goodbye to an old friend who has to move to a new town, we must shake hands, give a hug and a pat on the back (if you're Italian, you'll get a kiss on the cheek), and wave goodbye. The assignment must be submitted.

Submit with a smile.
Then celebrate. You did it. No worries, mate. Nothing you do now can make or break the assignment, so don't waste time stressing. Call it good, and move on.

And that's exactly what we're going to do, right now. We're going to move on to create, to write, while using all of the tips, tricks, and requisites in *Simplified Writing 101*. And, yes, the result leads to *success*.

I've thoroughly enjoyed our time together. Truly, completely, and absolutely enjoyed it. I hope you enjoyed it, too.

You know, I write for *you*. Not Joe down the street or Josephine across the globe. *You*, sitting here and reading these words on this page. For *you* can make a significant difference, through your writing. If you take the bits and pieces of knowledge from this book, put them together, and create your own artistic moments of writing, you will communicate clearly and powerfully.

Clear and powerful communication holds an incredible, miraculous amount of unreleased energy. You know, you might do more than get the "A" grade with your words. Through your writing skills, you might even become a world-changer.

With clear communication and the power of words behind you, within you, and before you, anything is possible.

Acknowledgements

Simplified Writing 101 was seven years in the making—a true labor of love. The content came from class time with my students—first, my students at Cornerstone University's *Professional and Graduate Studies Division* and, second, from my students in Patrick Henry College's writing courses. Thank you, students, for saying, "I wish I had an easier way to remember this stuff," and, "That needs to go in a book."

Thank you to all who gave feedback as the book was written. I may have taught you college-level writing, but you've taught me valuable lessons, too.

I thank my kids, especially the ones still at home…for all of the nights when bedtime hugs were given over the laptop and the hours of sitting next to me at coffee shops while I wrote and edited.

Finally, thank you to all the parents who kept asking for my live workshops to be put into a book. Here it is. I hope you enjoy this and all of the books in the *Simplified Writing* series.

Most of all, my prayer is that, through this book, your student becomes an excellent communicator of brilliant ideas. Because that's what good writing can do. And I think that's amazing.

About the Author

EB Conroy, MA, is the author of a number of books, including…

- *Simplified Writing 101: Top Secrets for College Success*
- *EB Conroy's Simplified Vocabulary Guide for College Writing Success*
- *20 Secrets to Success with Your Child; Wit and Wisdom from a Mom of 12*
- *"My Kid is Driving Me Crazy!" 14 Realistic Expectations that Make Parenting Easier*
- *40 Days to Balanced Parenting*
- *Why Should I Learn This? (co-editor)*
- *Miracle in the City of Angels (co-author)*
- *Matt's Pup (reader)*

For the past seven years, Erin has designed and taught *College-Level Writing Skills* and *Research and Writing* courses for Patrick Henry College, located in Purcellville, Virginia. For nine years previous, Conroy taught research, college-level composition, and business writing with Cornerstone University's Professional and Graduate Studies Division (for associate, bachelor, and masters students). At Cornerstone, Conroy also taught leadership and management; organizational development; motivational theory and practice; individual and group behavior; and health and wellness.

Along with teaching, Conroy has been designing online writing courses for middle school, high school, Advanced Placement (AP), and college for over ten years, including entire writing programs with close to 50 courses with beginning through advanced writing and rhetoric—and a 12-part online fiction writing program for teens. Professor Conroy's **TRUE NORTH READING: THE COMPLETE MASTERY READING AND SPELLING PROGRAM™**—*A* multi-sensory reading program for children— has been in development and testing since 1996 and can be found at www.TrueNorthReading.com.

In addition to creating reading and writing curricula, Conroy continues to write both non-fiction and fiction books. She completed a Master of Fine Arts (MFA) in Genre Fiction at Western State Colorado University and is a member of the Society for Children's Book Writers and Illustrators (SCBWI), American Christian Fiction Writers Association (ACFW), and Science Fiction and Fantasy Writers of America (SFWA). She has also spoken nationally regarding writing, education, and health. Conroy has also been quoted in print publications such as PARENTS and PARENTING magazines; been featured in hundreds of newspapers, including the CHICAGO TRIBUNE and DALLAS MORNING NEWS. Her words have appeared on hundreds of web sites. Featured on radio shows, she also speaks at live conventions and conferences.

Conroy lives in Michigan (USA), where she works from her home and home schools her youngest two teens.

Get the second book in the series...

- *EB Conroy's Simplified Vocabulary Guide for College Writing Success*

Coming soon

- *Simplified Research Writing*
- *Simplified Writing for Middle School Students*

Find Erin's books at Amazon.com today.

Why origami on the cover?

Origami is the craft of making beautiful shapes, designs, and creatures through paper folding. With one fold at a time, you can create something exquisite.

Writing is like that.

When you master one simple skill of writing, then add the skills together, you become an exquisite writer.

Read this book. Learn to "make the fold correctly." Put all of the folds together. And there you have it: clear, beautiful communication. Your ideas, out in the world.

Use *Simplified Writing* and make a difference.

EB Conroy, MA, MFA

Made in the USA
Middletown, DE
20 July 2024